PRIVIES GALORE

To my son,
Peter,
for all his love and understanding

PRIVIES GALORE

Mollie Harris

Have done with windy argument,
and let the matter drop.

Alan Sutton

First published in the United Kingdom in 1990
Alan Sutton Publishing Limited · Phoenix Mill · Far Thrupp · Stroud
Gloucestershire

First published in the United States of America in 1990
Alan Sutton Publishing Inc. · Wolfeboro Falls · NH 03896–0848

British Library Cataloguing in Publication Data
Harris, Mollie
Privies galore.
1. Great Britain, Lavatories, history
I. Title
696.1820941

ISBN 0-86299-752-6

Library of Congress Cataloging in Publication Data
applied for

Drawings by Martin Latham

Typeset in 11/16pt Imprint.
Typesetting and origination by
Alan Sutton Publishing Limited.
Printed in Great Britain by
Dotesios Printers Limited.

CONTENTS

ACKNOWLEDGEMENTS

Lots of people helped me in compiling this collection of privy gems, among them: Mrs J. Bentley; Mrs Bolton; Mrs Breton; Mavis Brown; Hugo Brunner; Sue Chapman; Margaret Cobb; Brian Durham; David Green; Harold Greening; Rachell Hayes; Joyce Latham; Douglas Mclean and Bill Tandy; Our Nev (*The Smokebox*); Millers Privy C.C.; The End (Leigh); Iona Opie; Oxford Archaeological Unit; Mr Penny; Priory Farm; Mr and Mrs Pullen; *Punch*; Jean Reynolds and sister; Mr R. Reynolds; A.H.T. Robb-Smith; Kate Rowe; Sir Steven Runciman; Mr Stringer; a councillor from Yarnton; Mrs Tavender; Michael Thomas; Mr and Mrs Tombs and friends; Mrs D. Walker.

To all my friends and to the many others I have not named, I offer my most grateful thanks for their stories, photographs (unfortunately not all the pictures I was sent could be used) and information, and for the many anecdotes and kindnesses offered to me while I was making this collection. Many thanks also to all the museums who kindly sent information, and special thanks to The Gladstone Pottery Museum at Stoke for permission to use items from their booklet.

The photographs on the following pages are by Sue Chapman: 1, 39, 42, 43, 68, 96, 98, 109, 112, 120, 122, 129, 131.

Mollie Harris

*Behind this door, made from old ship's timbers, was once a
three-holer privy*

INTRODUCTION

History has shown that in Britain Neolithic man simply walked away from his rubbish and body wastes when they became smelly and offensive, and just set up a home a bit further away.

Much later, in Norman times, pigs, geese and other domestic animals were allowed to foul the streets as they made their way out to pastures. In that period there were no sanitary arrangements for man either, so the streets and lanes in inhabited places became filthy and smelly, bringing diseases to many of the folk who lived there. But in 1388 the very first sanitary act in British history was passed by Parliament: 'The townsfolk themselves should remove from the streets, all the dirt and filth'. But this practice was not always carried out and often the 'filth' was deposited in the streets after dark.

And yet in the Palace of King Minos, at Knossos in ancient Crete, as far back as 2,000 BC, they had baths and fittings made of pottery, and a water supply that went through clay pipes. The latrines, too, had a water supply with wooden seats and earthenware pans, and evidence of this is still visible today.

It is believed that the Romans took the idea of a sanitary

Were these ancient remains on Kos ever used as privies?

system from Knossos, and built on it, creating their wonderful aqueducts all over their great empire, supplying their people with running water for baths and latrines – and drains to take away the waste. Even the thousands of Roman soldiers along Hadrian's Wall – the construction of which was started in AD 120 – eventually had all these comforts. At some of the 'stations' along the Wall, they built latrines where twenty men could sit at one time. And in many of the Roman cities they built public latrines with marble seats, often formed in a semi-circle over a stream or other water supply. The latrines became meeting places for further discussion as well as a 'place of easement'. Often there was a channel of water in the front of the latrines, where the users dipped the sponge-sticks that were used instead of lavatory paper, which was not introduced until very much later (and indeed is still not used in many parts of the world). History tells us that there were, in fact, over one hundred and forty public latrines in Rome by AD 315, and when the legions left our shores their villas, fitted with baths and under-floor heating and water-controlled privies, remained: but much of this was forgotten, and it was centuries before these things were once again widely used in Britain.

In the thirteenth century, stone-seated privies were built into castle walls, and the contents slipped down the stones of these walls and then into the moat below. Owners of some castles years later built a sort of channel that went from the privy itself right to the bottom of the building, thus shielding from sight the great brown stain that had been made previously! The contents then dropped down this stone channel either into a moat below or into a huge cesspit. There are the remains of two of this latter type at Broughton Castle, near Banbury, the Home of Lord and Lady Saye and Sele. They are what Lord Saye and Sele terms as 'straight drop' privies, and although the seating arrangement has long since disappeared, both the little room above and the stone-built channel on the castle wall are still intact (see page 4).

Believe it or not, in London in the fourteenth century, there were only three public privies or latrines: one at Temple Bridge, built over the River Thames, one at Queenshithe, and a third on London Bridge – which meant that 2,000 tons of human waste had to be disposed of each year into the Thames. In 1309 one of the first bridges was built over the river, and the saying was then,

3

'Straight drop' privy and stone channel at Broughton Castle

'that the bridge was built for wise men to go over and fools to go under'.

The resulting stench from the Thames made it very bad for the people who lived on the riverside, especially in the summertime. And at the Houses of Parliament, sheets perfumed with lavender and roses were draped over the windows to try to 'stay' the terrible smell that rose up from the Thames. It was not until after the Black Death in 1348, in which almost half the population of England was wiped out, that people became less likely to discharge their sewage into rivers: huge cesspits were built in the cities which, of course, had to be cleaned out quite frequently by 'gongfermors' ('gong' from the Saxon *gang*, mean-

*Stool-type conveniences amassed by Carl Gustav Wrangel in
the seventeenth century (from* Country Life, *1985)*

ing 'to go off' and 'fermor' from *fey*, 'to cleanse').

Then there was a long period when royalty and the landed
gentry had the 'close stool' type of convenience placed in several
rooms in their palaces and mansions. These were box-like
contraptions, often with seats covered in velvet or other soft
material, under which were fitted buckets to be emptied daily by
their servants. And at this time the poor country folk would have
been advised to go and relieve themselves out in the fields, 'a
bow-shot away' from their humble dwellings.

In the sixteenth century, Sir John Harrington, a member of

Queen Elizabeth's court, invented a water closet with a flushing system. First he installed one in his own house at Kelston near Bath. Then he wrote a book on the subject called *A Metamorphosis of Ajax* (Ajax being another word for privy), which was published in 1596. Queen Elizabeth was not amused by this, and disapproved of the book, consequently Harrington was, for a time, banned from the court. But eventually the Queen forgave him and then he installed a water closet for her at Richmond Palace, and a copy of the book hung up in there. And although Harrington's closet was called 'A privy of perfection', it really lacked many present-day standards, but was indeed in advance of any other closet of that time. Unfortunately the idea didn't take on in other circles. This was probably because of the lack of running water, so once again things slipped back to the old ways of relieving oneself: the rich to their 'close stools' and the peasants to the fields.

It was not until 1775 that a man called Alexander Cummings invented a patent closet bowl that held water, which was operated by a sort of lever. The action of keeping the water in the bowl was done by the means of a sliding valve that also admitted water from the cistern. (The word 'valve' comes from the Latin word *valvus*, meaning 'door').

Then in 1777 Lemuel Prosser patented a pump-operated closet, but his invention wasn't a great success. The force-pump closet had a large vertical cylinder at the back with a handle that could lift a piston. The rising piston would draw out the contents of the pan into the upright cylinder. As soon as the piston was pushed down, the hinged valve also stayed down and the pressure opened a valve in the side, forcing wastes into the soil pipe. Mr Prosser had had something like this in mind in 1777, but the first workable design was that of Jonathan Downton of Blackwall whose 'forcing-pump', patented in 1825, was reputed to have the sturdiness of a ship's pump – which was hardly surprising since Downton was a shipwright.

Towards the end of the eighteenth century Joseph Bramah came on the 'closet scene' and patented a water closet with two hinged valves, one of the valves allowed water from the cistern and the other was fixed under the lavatory pan: this valve reserved a quantity of water in the pan which helped to prevent the smell rising back up from the soil pipe.

For a while there seemed to be a lull in clever inventions, until, in the mid-nineteenth century, the coming of the 'earth closets'. These had portable wooden frames and seats with a hopper at the back which was filled with dry earth or ashes, and a bucket underneath. The user simply pulled a handle which released a layer of the earth from the hopper, which fell on to the contents of the bucket and made things much more pleasant for the next user – and cut down the smell, too. These types were used inside houses, schools and prisons. The creator of these closets (which he patented in 1860) was The Reverend Henry Moule, who lived in the village of Fordington in Dorset. Conditions here for the poorer classes were very bad, and smallpox, typhus and scarlet fever resulting from the poor sanitation were responsible for many deaths. During his time there, Revd Moule did much to improve the lot of the villagers. He was awarded £500 – an enormous sum in those days – by the

Secretary of State for India, where his invention was very widely used. And Moule's closets were still being sold as late as 1908 at the Army and Navy Stores, for thirty shillings each.

Soon after Moule had patented his earth closet, John Parker, a Woodstock cabinet-maker, came up with an improvement. John Parker's earth closet was fully automatic: when the user rose, pressure-activated levers released the earth or ashes automatically. In spite of this it is Moule rather than Parker who is remembered for the invention of this very sophisticated type of closet.

In 1886 Charles Richardson came up with the following specification – strictly for those living in a rural area!

DRY PRIVY
Minimum Size,
FOR A COTTAGE

Built with 9-in. brick walls, and brick on edge flooring, 4ft. 6in. by 3 ft. in the clear, as shown on the Drawing. It will take 4 cubic yards of brickwork, and may be built for about £5.

A *dry* privy may also be safely built as a lean-to against the back wall of the Cottage, by which means the cost of the front wall will be saved. The door will then be on the side. The back should, in *all* cases, join to a garden bed.

It must always be borne in mind that the *essential* features of the 'Dry Privy' are: firstly, that the droppings should be kept DRY, and secondly, that they should be kept ABOVE the surface soil.

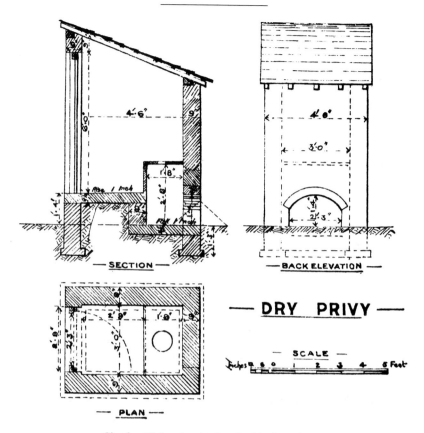

Charles Richardson's plan for his dry privy

For this purpose the floor of the Privy is raised two steps above the ground level, in order to form a 'catch' behind *at* ground level; the floor of this catch should slope slightly outwards, so that any moisture should naturally drain that way into a small heap of earth which has been tipped against the archway at the back.

9

The result of this arrangement is, that we are coming back again to Nature, who has provided the surface soil to catch and purify all these things. We thus avoid entirely the formation of *Sewage*, and the consequent pollution of our wells, water-springs and rivers, and the propagation of fevers and zymotic diseases in general.

The Dry Privy requires no looking after, and is never offensive; all that it requires is that it should be emptied once in six months or so, and this is done without trouble in five minutes, when the earth and the droppings are shovelled out *on the level* and mixed together with a little more earth, after which a barrow full of fresh earth is tipped against the archway, and that is all that is wanted. If what has been taken out is left in a heap for two or three weeks it becomes a valuable manure for the garden.

Old-fashioned privies, instead of having the floor raised two steps above the surface, in order to form a 'catch', usually have *cess-pits* dug into the ground; these are a mistake, for they hold water, and thus form *Sewage*, which makes the privy very offensive and sometimes the cause of the propagation of fevers round about them; besides making the emptying of them a very difficult and offensive operation. But the evils of these are as nothing compared with those of the water-closet.

CHARLES RICHARDSON,

June, 1886   10 Berkeley Square.

On the whole, people came to prefer closets using water.

There were many types of these, ranging from those which were strategically placed to take advantage of a running water supply to ones requiring ingenious and complicated contraptions which could have been devised by Heath Robinson. The former were often the simpler to use (and sometimes, one imagines, by far the safer!), but they did have their problems. In monasteries they seemed to have quite a good system. Their privies were usually built over streams to ensure good drainage, with seats partitioned off so that each occupant could do what he had to do in private. At Tintern Abbey, the Severn tide, says Reginald Reynolds:

> was ingeniously employed to effect a complete flushing of monastic dykes that must surely have swept the monkes from their seats when the tide was at its highest.

Perhaps they made a 'habit' of going at low tide only!

From Ipswich comes this story:

> I have just read an article about a privy built over a stream – I have not only seen one, but used one, in Devon.
>   Friends of mine bought a neglected farm on the edge of Exmoor. I was directed out of the front door into the walled garden. On one side was a door. I went in and there was a

A miller's privy astride a stream

three-holer scrubbed white. On lifting the lid I saw, many
feet below, a fast-running stream. It was a queer sensation,
and although my host had made many enquiries no one
could trace where the stream went to.

It makes you wonder . . .

Another simple system is described by a lady from Yeovil, in
Somerset:

At the farm where I was brought up, we had a two-seater
privy which was about twenty yards up the garden path. It
had one large hole for adults and another about half the size
which I and my sisters and four brothers used. Like many
other farms we had a pond, which was close to the privy. At
a convenient height there were cavities in the privy wall and
when the pond became full it over-flowed through the
cavities and took much of the contents of the privy with it,
and then it went into a ditch – and finally out into a stream.
I have no recollection of it ever receiving any other
attention.

And then of course there were semi-natural systems of
flushing, like the one in use in the early 1930s at Handborough

JENNINGS'
PATENT TILT-UP AND LIPPED LAVATORY,
For Hospitals, Barracks, Asylums, Schools, Stations, Unions, and Buildings of every Class.

The Honorary Testimonial and MEDAL of THE SOCIETY OF ARTS, and the EXHIBITION PRIZE MEDAL of 1851, were awarded to GEORGE JENNINGS, for his various PATENTED SANITARY INVENTIONS.

The simplicity of this arrangement, its freedom from complication, and efficiency, have caused it to be generally adopted.

In Hospitals and other Public Buildings the deposit left on Basins drained through a small plug-hole is not only objectionable, but is considered by Medical Men to be often the means of communicating disease.

In a sanitary point of view these Lavatories are much to be preferred, as the contents, after use, are thrown direct from the Basin, by tilting it as shown in the Illustration. The lowering of it to its former position ensures a fresh and ample supply of Water.

ENGINEERING AND SANITARY DEPÔT,
HOLLAND STREET, BLACKFRIARS ROAD, LONDON, S.E.

Every appliance tending to Health and Comfort may be seen in operation at the above Works.

station, in Oxfordshire, on the Worcester line. Here the water for the ladies' lavatory came from the rain water tank: when it was very rainy it flooded the place out, but during the summer, when it was fine for weeks, there was no water at all for flushing!

Then there were the slop water or 'tipper' closets, such as those described in Gladstone Pottery Museum's pamphlet *The Past & Present*:

In areas where water was not plentiful or in towns where there was a strong objection to a large expenditure of water, slop closets using waste water from the kitchen sink were devised and adopted. Some, like that patented by T. Lister in 1859, required the water to be released from a cistern, but the 'tipper' closet of the second half of the nineteenth century operated automatically by means of a tilting bucket which tilted or tipped the moment it was full of slop water from the kitchen. These closets were sturdily practical. One maker claimed that they never froze in winter, which was probably quite true, and J. and A. Duckett, in a patent of 1892, refer to a 'quatrefoil-shaped passage to arrest salmon tins'.

It is said that one of the first persons to introduce or advocate slop closets on a large scale was Dr Alfred Hill of Birmingham. The best known types of tipper closets were made by such firms as Duckett, Allen or Day. Waste water closets seem to have been used a great deal in Lancashire and Yorkshire. Tipper closets, with their characteristic turret-like pedestal of brown stoneware,

were in use for a century. Around 1890 slop water closets were being recommended in Longton as being suitable for cottage properties. A child visiting a grandparent at a farm in the Staffordshire Moorlands in the 1930s, was later to recall the sudden subterranean din of this closet as a spooky memory. One or two were still in use in 1981.

Some of the men who patented WCs, when pan closets, washdown closets, hopper closets and long hopper closets – and many others – came on the market, were: George Jennings, T.W. Twyford, John Gaittait, William Law. But we in the country still used our old vault privies well into the twentieth century, and in some areas buckets are *still* being used.

Another popular development was the 'trough' or 'range' closet. Originally the trough closet was a channel of glazed earthenware or stoneware, through which water could flow or be flushed. Usually set up for schools or factories, it had a line of wooden seats over it. Water could be directed into it by an attendant or, splashingly, noisily and alarmingly, by an automatic syphon cistern. It was wasteful as well as unhygienic.

Later versions of the trough closet include the range closet which was basically a series of pans over a common horizontal drainpipe with a flush and an S-trap at one end. Some pans used in these systems were of a syphonic type.

Living as I did in a small village in the 1920s meant that I was brought up in a world of privies, earth closets, or vaults, as some folk called them. Everybody in the village had one. Well, some of the big houses had two, one for 'them' and one for the servants and gardeners.

The privies of my youth ranged from one-holers, two-holers, three-ers and four-ers, and when I first started to make enquiries about privies in the village where I live now, an old fellow said to me, 'You should 'a writ that book fifty years ago, thur used to be a five-oler in ower village'. A five-holer! Can you imagine that five people from one family would all want to go at the same time? I mean nowadays, even if you have a big family you are lucky if you have two lavatories, one up and one down.

These days we shut ourselves away and get on with our ablutions in private. But when we were young we often used to go down to our two-holer with brothers and sisters, and even the next-door neighbour's children. And it wasn't always just for 'business'. Oh, no! You lingered there for ages, to chat and giggle perhaps about a local boy who you fancied. And the smell that was always prevalent never seemed to bother us at all. We also found sanctuary down there, an escape from washing-up or taking younger brothers for walks out of our mother's way. On the other hand, if you could sneak down there on your own, it was lovely, away from the crowded cottage. You could just sit there, with the door three parts open, and the sun shining on your legs – to read from the squares of newspaper (the 'bum fodder' as we called it), or watch the birds in the hedge that separated us from one of the other cottages. There you could dream or have a quiet cry in secret: it was a peaceful place, until a shout from one of the family who was desperate to use the privy shattered your peace!

And I vividly remember, when we were young, we had oranges *only* at Christmas time. Two each, always, in our stockings. And in those days the oranges were wrapped in fine orange sort of tissue paper; we used to smooth it out carefully and use it when we went to the old privy. For two days we were in heaven! It was such a luxury, and a nice change from newspaper or *Old Moore's Almanack*.

Our privy also offered sanctuary for the spiders who wove huge magical webs down there. One old lady from the village used to come and ask my mother if she had any black cobwebs – good for stemming the blood, she reckoned. She never asked missus-next-door for any: no cobweb ever had the chance to survive in her privy. My mother and the old lady would toddle off in search of these old black cobwebs (they had to be old ones) either in the privy or in the old wash-house which was a few yards from the cottage, and the old woman would go off pleased as punch with half a dozen cobwebs wrapped up in a bit of old newspaper.

Of course the spiders lived there because of the flies and the flies lived there because of the smells and the rich pickings. I can't remember ever going down there – at least during the warm weather – and not finding a dozen or more 'blue-assed flies' buzzing about in there, especially when the six-monthly visit of the lavendar cart was due: our privy, with nine people using it, got a bit on the full side.

One for Dad, Mum and child!

Some of the village privies were spotless. 'You could eat your dinner off some of the seats, they be that clean,' missus-next-door said one day. 'Who the devil would want to?' my mother cried. You see, missus-next-door only had one child, and our mother had seven, so you couldn't expect ours to be like the Crystal Palace, even if hers was.

It was well into the thirties before some of the village privies, including ours, were changed to buckets – which was supposed to be a 'leap forward in hygiene'.

'Hygiene, my foot,' our mother retorted when a local councillor said this to her. 'You don't know what you're talking about,' she went on, 'there's nine of us using that so-called hygienic bucket – so what happens with my big, healthy, growing family visiting the privy at least twice a day, the damned bucket's full and running over by night-time, so it has to be emptied and the contents buried. The only blessing,' she went on, 'is that we shan't have to bother about manuring the garden, it'll be done for us.'

And 'twas true, we and other villagers produced what Old Fred used to call 'jynourmus' vegetables.

A fine back-to-back garden privy

Fruit of Our Labours

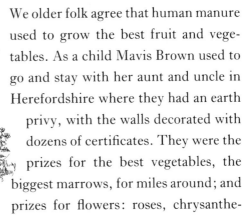

We older folk agree that human manure used to grow the best fruit and vegetables. As a child Mavis Brown used to go and stay with her aunt and uncle in Herefordshire where they had an earth privy, with the walls decorated with dozens of certificates. They were the prizes for the best vegetables, the biggest marrows, for miles around; and prizes for flowers: roses, chrysanthemums and many others. Mavis used to sit there entranced, reading them: first prize for almost everything. When she asked her aunt why she pinned them up in the privy, her aunt replied: 'Well, what comes out of the privy goes on the garden to grow the fruit, vegetables and flowers that wins us the certificates, so I reckon that's where they should be, where the credit lies.'

One old fellow who knew that I 'collected' privy stories told me this:

Snug in an English garden

A visitor arrived at a lonely farmhouse one day. He had been invited to have a meal with the occupants, but first he asked where the privy was. He made his way down the yard to the little house, and looked down the hole where the water was rushing through to see a duck swimming along the channel.

Back at the farmhouse, his smiling host rubbed his hands together and said, 'I do hope you enjoy your meal. It's duck, one of our own.' Quick as a flash, the guest replied, 'Oh, I *am* sorry, I'm afraid I'm allergic to duck!'

And a friend of mine who married a French girl just before the outbreak of World War II, told me of his first visit to her home.

When he asked where the lavatory was, he was told, 'Oh, you just go out in the orchard, find an apple tree and do it under it.' He was doubly surprised to find that the hens that were running about in the orchard promptly ate what he had done.

'I took particular notice not to eat any of their eggs while I was there,' he said.

One man who knew the value of the contents of the earth closet was Frank Truffle. In the village pub one night, he was telling a man from the City about the days when they had an earth privy and used the contents on the garden. 'Ah,' he said, 'we growed some wonderful crops they days. Taters as big as footballs and marrows as long as wheelbarrows.'

He would have agreed with my old shepherd friend, Mont Abbott. When he moved from his old cottage, where he had a bucket lavatory, to one where there was a modern water one, I asked him what he thought of his new 'little house'. He said, 'Well, 'tis alright, but I'll bet we'll never get fust prize for marrows again.'

Another man who made the most of 'solid waste' was Harry Pearson. He was in charge of the local sewage works. In his spare time he cultivated a fair strip of land attached to the works, using the 'solid' waste, after the liquid had been pumped off, to manure the ground. He grew some splendid crops which he sold to the local shops. But what he made most of his money on was the free crop of tomatoes which came up every year of their own accord. What happened was, folks in the town were eating tomatoes and the seeds went through them, finally ending up on Harry's allotment. They were, everybody agreed, the best tasting tomatoes for miles around.

A deserted Elsan at Whittington, Gloucestershire

The 'hanging loo' at Priory Farm

One day I was invited by the owners of Priory Farm in the Cotswolds to visit their home, where they have two privies, one inside and one out. They call the inside one 'the hanging loo' and as you can see by the photograph opposite, it literally hangs on the wall of the house. It was one of the earliest 'flush' lavatories. Rain water from the guttering around the house was directed straight into the lavatory pan, so no pull chain was needed. The water and contents of it went straight into a large pipe, which is also the only outward means of holding up this small building. From there the contents were piped underground and into one of the six ponds that were once in the grounds.

But that wasn't the only thing that flowed into the ponds. High up in the Cotswold hills, about a mile from the farm, is a lovely spring that flows down into the valley. The land once belonged to a monastic order and by a little diversion the monks, years and years ago, put the spring to very good use. From down the hillside it rushes through a culvert near to the house – and there, on its first job, it flows through a two-holer: the owner calls this 'a rushing flush', for that is just what the spring does. All the contents were swept from there through a lead pipe (still visible) and on into the cheese room and dairy: I guess the monks were limited to special times to visit the two-holer otherwise it might have complicated things in the cheese room! From there the water was diverted underground to the ponds, which in the early days would have been full of carp and other fish that would have gone towards feeding the monks. The water then went on the drive of their flour mill, before finally flowing into the River Severn.

And Margaret Cobb, in her *Recollection*, tells us the following:

27

Privies side by side

Wolvercote was a potentially very unhealthy place, particularly during my early years, as there was no sewerage before 1939. Indeed . . . some human excrement simply landed up in the river. The Victoria County History says that in 1952 Oxford's sewerage system was 'probably the most backward in the country'; it seems amazing that there weren't outbreaks of typhus. You could have had sewerage installed privately in 1930, but that would have cost £100, which was a huge amount of money in those days, and most people simply did not have it.

Mr Allen – 'Wally' – was exempt from the First World

War for doing 'work of national importance', which, in his case, was dealing with sewage disposal in the village of Wolvercote. He, with an employee, would go around the village with an old two-wheeled, horse-drawn, tin cart, which used to swing from side to side. They would go down to the privies at the bottom of the gardens and empty the contents into the cart which, slopping copiously to and fro, they would then take to fields rented from Red Barn Farm, which was on the way to Woodstock.

According to Mrs Godwin, some local people were afraid that her father used to grow vegetables on this land and when she used to go round the village with her fathers horse and cart they would eye her dubiously, asking, 'Did your father grow these, dear?' If the answer was in the affirmative, they would reply 'Well . . . not today, thank you'.

At one farmhouse that I visited in a small village called Leigh, in Gloucestershire, there was still part of quite a large moat, where the contents of one of the two earth privies went. The privy was built on the side of the moat. It had a stone chute where the faeces slipped down: this little chute even had a small slate roof which

The privy at Leigh where the contents went into the moat . . .

. . . and where, for generations, members of the family would sign their names

would have shielded the muck from the inhabitants. The privy was named by the family 'The End'. The words were boldly painted on the door. Inside on a sort of backboard of the privy, members of the family have for generations signed their names.

The owner told me that for many years the family had been one of the country's biggest suppliers of goldfish – the finest in the land. Evidently they thrived on the privy offerings.

A smart indoor privy in an old farmhouse

A FONDNESS FOR

FRESH AIR

It's funny, how some folk these days screw up their noses when earth closets are mentioned. Why is it, then, that they are remembered so vividly and with a sort of affection? And think of all the humorous stories that have been remembered, the accidents and happenings in connection with the privies of yester-year. And how lovingly David Green wrote about his earth closet, in his book *Country Neighbours*:

No indoor lavatory meant, among other things, a blow of fresh air, whatever the weather. In summer it had the attractions of a gardener's bothy, our lilac-shaded privy, and it made a capital place for musing on the garden's crops: or,

This Cotswold stone building at Nympsfield houses a two-holer in good condition

with its view of bird-box and the birds that foraged among the beansticks (including a lesser-spotted woodpecker), was it to be scorned as an ornithologist's hide. There was also the wren that nested behind the door.

There were drawbacks, of course. The privy might get snowed up entirely overnight, or a passing soldier in the weighty accoutrements of battle ('readin' and smokin' and makin' a weddin' of it', as a commiserator guessed) might, and in fact did, break the seat clean in two, but neither mishap was irremediable, and although I did the spadework myself I decided, at least when the damson was in bloom and the mistle-thrush singing in the orchard, that I wouldn't change places with anyone, no not with the most sumptuously porcelained and mahoganied millionaire.

Joyce Bentley wrote this in a Women's Institute magazine of January 1985:

Our lavatory was twenty yards from the house, high on the moors with nothing but three gappy stone walls and a plan door between us and the Irish Sea. When gale-force winds blew in from the east they whipped the door open when we least expected it, and when they blew from the west we could hardly open the door to get out. When it snowed we had to dig our way in and then brush the snow off the seat when it had drifted.

When it rained we stood in an inch of water and only managed to keep the toilet tissue dry by wrapping it in a polythene bag. In the autumn we were ankle deep in leaves, and in the summer – oh, the bats! Attracted by the light of the lantern they whirred noiselessly about our heads.

Ours was a pail closet, you understand, set in a wooden bench with a hole in the top. There was a small door at the side of the wall to enable the disposal engineers to insert a hook into the handle of the pail and drag it out for emptying into the green tanker provided for the purpose.

It doesn't sound *totally* idyllic, but isn't there a touch of wistfulness about this story?

When there was talk of water closets being installed in a Cotswold village, one old lady was heard to remark, 'I shall stick to my old earth closet, that damp water in them newfangled 'uns would give I the piles quicker than anything.'

For others, the privy at the bottom of the garden offered boundless social possibilities. I was told the following story by the local postman, while holidaying in Wales one year:

A mother, father and their young son went to live in a small village in Wales. The lad was very shy and wouldn't mix with the other children. Living next door was a nice young girl, but the lad wouldn't even say hello to her. His mother tried to encourage him to be friendly with the girl, and said

A fine sea view on a Greek island!

to him, 'Next time she goes out into the yard, go and have a few words with her.'

Next day he saw the girl going down to the privy, so he waited until she came out and then went up to her and very briefly spoke to her. Then he rushed, blushing furiously, into the cottage.

'Well,' his mother said, 'what did you say to her?'

The lad replied, 'I just said "Had a good shit then, Blodwen, did you?" But she never said anything.'

Knowing my interest in privies, Mr Michael Thomas, the Director of Avoncroft Museum in Stoke Heath, Bromsgrove, asked me to re-open one they had just acquired. Delightedly I

Remains of the privy at Yarnton Rectory near Oxford

Inside the privy at Avoncroft Museum

said yes. I was assisted by the Managing Director of *Portaloo*, Mr Francis Celoria – it was his company who had helped to pay for the restoration of the eighteenth-century privy.

This very fine ancient three-holer was rescued from a garden of a grand house, which was situated in Leominster, on the border of Herefordshire and Shropshire. The privy was taken down brick-by-brick and board-by-board, re-erected and restored.

When I turned the key in the lock to declare the privy open, I had a surprise! Unbeknown to me – and to the crowd who had gathered for the opening – inside, sitting on the seats, were three people: Ron and Anne Andrews and their daughter, beautifully dressed in eighteenth-century clothes.

*A good example of a solid Scottish privy, with a hole for emptying,
from Fife*

The three holes, two for grown-ups and one smaller hole for a
child, were set in a box-like bench over a very deep cesspit, and
the only way to empty it was through a large trap door in the
floor in front of the row of seats.

The building itself is quite big, as privies go, and has lovely
decorative panelling in the wall facing the seating arrangement,
with a sash window either side of the glazed door. When it was in
its original setting, the occupants sitting there in their splendour
would have had a delightful view of the garden.

PRIVIES GALORE
OR WHAT GOES IN . . .

One of the nastiest aspects of privies was the emptying of them. In the vicinity of Stoke-on-Trent – and doubtless elsewhere in the country – there were, in the 1880s and 1890s, some rather basic privies that would have shocked the reformers of the 1940s. These closets were no more than a large, round-bottomed cylinder of stoneware, rather more than a metre high. The cylinder was made in two parts, being joined at the flanged collar two-thirds of the way up which rested the vessel on a tiled floor. On the top was a wood bench with a hole in it, and little more . . . When the receptacle was offensively full, the arrival of the soil collector from the corporation would be anxiously awaited, since he would ladle the contents out.

One such closet was last emptied in March 1980, just in time for a Gladstone Pottery Museum team to recover the privy. The

*Outside the 'parson's privy' at Yarnton Rectory: the hopper for ashes
or earth . . .*

. . . and inside: note the home-made toilet paper holder

location was Coalpit Hill, Talke, near Kidsgrove, Newcastle-under-Lyme, in Staffordshire.

The following is a report by Dr Samuel Rideal, written in 1901, on the 'pail system':

In Rochdale and some other northern towns, the excreta are collected in iron or tarred oak pails of a capacity of about two cubic feet and provided with lids. They are placed under the seat of the closet which should be well ventilated, and the contents are covered with cinders or ashes and removed at least once a week, a clean pail being substituted. It is important that the contents should be kept as dry as possible, and that if it is designed to convert the matter afterwards into manure, nothing but the excreta and a minimum of ash should be thrown into the pail.

In some villages the pail system is carried out in a much less careful manner, the pails being collected at night-time . . . and the contents, called 'night soil', were emptied into ditches and pits and covered with soil (earth).

One man, contributing to a recent issue of the little magazine *The Smokebox*, writes:

One very important craft known to the true countryman is that of 'Bucketeering', and I am proud to say that I was apprenticed to this skill together with my younger brother. Our dad was the master and a highly skilled tutor of this ancient skill.

A short-handled 'shituss scoop' – or is it broken?

The tools of the trade can be either a yoke (as used by milkmaids) or a solid two-wheeled truck.

To become proficient as a 'Bucketeer', you need to reside in accommodation that does not boast a WC and is not remotely connected to mains sewage, and at the same time has no back or front garden of any consequence, and no cesspool.

So what do we have? Why, a 'Country Privy', resplendent with sloping corrugated iron roof and an outward-opening door on a piece of string.

Now disposing of the contents is where the skill comes in. Timing is critical: the receptacle should not be too full because of weight, but full enough so as not to have to make more trips than is necessary.

I rented a piece of ground adjacent to my twelve-pole allotment where burying could be carried out with full military honours. This was about eight hundred yards from our house.

When we were all at home (six of us), this task, needless to say, required attention at least twice a week.

So after issuing warnings to the household that the privy was closed it fell to my brother and myself to 'dispose' of the contents.

The idea was to open the side door of the privy and remove the large bucket, shaped something like a First World War German helmet (without the spike) or an old fashioned coal scuttle.

Now if everyone had been 'on form' over the past few

days and your timing was twenty-four hours out one had to approach this with great caution.

Once the receptacle was clear of the privy my brother (because he was smaller in stature than I) would manoeuvre the truck as close as possible, then I, standing with legs slightly apart, with one upward haul would lift the receptacle high enough for the truck to be pushed forward and the load lowered carefully on to the one-inch floorboards of this conveyance. The whole unit was then covered with a piece of canvas or sack.

Unloading was a reverse of the loading but a lot more hazardous because of the upward lift: if the truck was pulled away too quickly it caught the base rim of the bucket and tipped the contents into the top of the bearer's wellingtons, which always caused a great deal of mirth from the 'truck puller' and a lot of swearing from the loader. On numerous occasions I had to wash my feet and socks in the water hole before going home or I would have been ostracized.

The other aspect of timing was the time of day. If it was a Sunday you had to make it between Holy Communion and Morning Prayer, to avoid meeting as many people as possible.

I remember one Sunday, a hiking party of about thirty young ladies between the ages of eighteen and twenty-two was passing through the village. Just as we were at the point of no return my brother dropped the shafts to the truck and bolted, leaving me feeling a right burke with the truck and

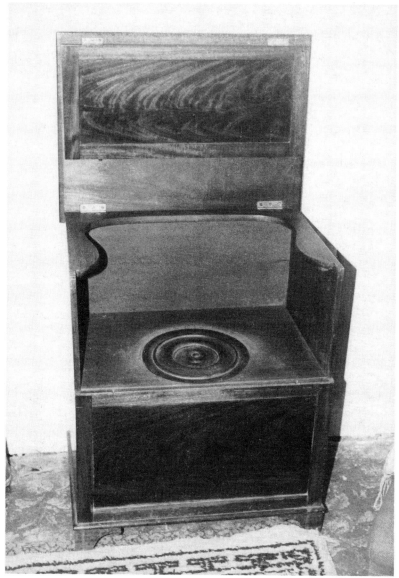

Found in the bedroom of an old lady's house

load. I pulled my cap down over my eyes and looked down at the road in front of me, and shame upon shame the leader, a very attractive woman, said, 'Excuse me, is this the right way to Cowley?' I grunted, 'Yes, turn left at the crossroads.' As the last of the party was passing one of them remarked, 'What's that funny smell?', to which her friend replied, 'Oh, I think it's something to do with the chemical they put in the soil!'

On another very embarrassing occasion, I was on my own and I had just gone under the railway bridge, which is built on an S-bend, and the blasted axle broke, tipping the truck on its side. Well, what do you do in a case like that? You can't abandon it because you need the bucket – and you can't carry it the other quarter mile. I had to face the indignity of standing there whilst the upper crust of the community passed me on their way to church. I felt like a leper – they all crossed to the other side of the road.

At last a chap I knew saw the position I was in, and rode off on his bike to report to my dad and a relief truck was brought out and the job completed. Ah yes, I suppose they were happy days but even so I find it much more satisfying to press a lever and 'hey presto!', it's gone. But at least I am an indentured 'Bucketeer'.

Of course, most of the stories connected with privies happen to come from the country areas, and a man from Chipping Campden in Gloucestershire told me this tale:

My brother Ruffy and I were delivering fish around the villages in a pony and trap. Ruffy was a bit of a dealer and was always on the lookout for a bargain. We got to Badger Brook Farm and he told the farmer's wife that he wanted to buy a good cockerel. They were all running about the farmyard. 'Go and take your pick', she told him. He spied a good one and went chasing after him.

Well, unbeknown to him, the privy had been emptied the day before and the contents spread over the garden, but with plenty of ashes and cinders scattered over the top. The cockerel shot across the cinders – and so did Ruffy!

My goy! he was in a state! We was soon up in that old trap and off home damned quick. Our mother made him strip in the yard and we chucked buckets of water over him to get the worst off. Then he had to sit wrapped up in an old blanket, while the water in the old copper (in the wash-house) got hot enough for him to have a bath in the old tin bath out there.

And just to prove that things are – or at least, were – the same the world over, here is a 'dunny' story from Australia, but I admit I don't know who wrote it:

Ever since I could remember, the dunny man had come running down the driveway once a week. From inside the house, we could hear his running footsteps. Then we could hear the rattle and thump as he lifted the lavatory lid, took out the full pan, clipped on a special lid, and set down an

An old Aussie dunny

empty pan in its place. After more rattling and banging, there was an audible intake of breath as he hefted the full pan on to his shoulder. Then the footsteps went back along the driveway, slower this time but still running. From outside in the street there was rattling, banging and shouting as the full pan was loaded on to the dunny cart along with all the other full pans.

I often watched the dunny cart from the front window. As it slowly made its noisome way down the street, the dunny men ran to and from it with awesome expertise. They wore shorts, sandshoes, and nothing else except a suntan suspiciously deep on the forearms. Such occasional glimpses were all one was allowed by one's parents and all that was encouraged even by the dunny men themselves. They preferred to work in nobody's company except their own. They were a band apart.

The situation tolerated by Mr Greening's grandparents in the Cotswolds, was rather worse. Their cottage was one in a row of six all adjoining, with no back way. And when their privy needed to be emptied – which was about once every two years – his grandfather would ask a fellow called Harry Maisey to do it. 'Course this was always a winter-time job because of the smell and the flies. All the contents of the privy had to be wheeled in a wheelbarrow, first down the garden path and then right through the cottage, and dumped outside close up against the cottage wall. There were no footpaths in those days.

And there it stayed, with a few ashes sprinkled over it, to make it a bit better for passers-by, until the coalman had finished his rounds. Then the coalman would shovel the privy contents into the coal cart and take it away to some old pit well out of the town.

During the 'bucket age', some of the bucket collectors would walk ahead of the 'lavender' or 'violet' cart. They would then walk through the cottages to collect the full buckets, but if the weather was bad the men would sit down in the kitchens, with the full buckets beside them, to wait for the cart to arrive. The men were sometimes offered a cup of tea and a bit of cake, which they readily accepted . . .

However, of all the emptyings I've heard of, I think that Smollett's description in *Humphrey Clinker*, written in 1771, is the worst:

And now, dear Mary, we have got to Haddinborrough, (Edinburgh) among the Scots, who are civil enuff for our money, thof I don't speak their lingo. But they should not go for to impose upon foreigners; for the bills in their houses say, they have different easements to let; and behold there is nurro geaks in the whole kingdom, nor any thing for poor sarvants, but a barrel with a pair of tongs thrown a-cross; and all the chairs in the family are emptied into this here barrel once a-day; and at ten o'clock at night the whole cargo is flung out of a back windore that looks into some street or lane, and the maid calls gardy loo* to the

---

* *Gardy loo.* Scoto-French for *'gare à l'eau'*, 'ware water'.

passengers, which signifies Lord have mercy upon you. and this is done every night in every house in Haddinborrough . . .

Compare with this Bartoline Saddletree's account of the case 'about a servitude of waterdrap', arising out of the Highland maid-servant's having 'made that gardyloo out of the wrang window, out of respect for twa Highlandmen that were speaking Gaelic in the close before the right ane' (Sir Walter Scott: *The Heart of Midlothian*, Chap. XXVI). And, from the same book, this comment:

> You are no stranger to their method of discharging all their impurities from their windows, at a certain hour of the night as the custom is in Spain, Portugal, and some part of France and Italy – a practice to which I can by no means be reconciled; for notwithstanding all the care that is taken by their scavengers to remove this nuisance every morning by break of day, enough still remains to offend the eyes, as well as other organs of those whom use has not hardened against all delicacy of sensation.

THE PROBLEM
WITH PRIVIES

When I was walking the Cotswold Way, I met a charming old couple who lived just outside Dursley, and this is what they told me:

We got the electric *and* a water lavatory now, but we had one of them earth ones right away from the house for years.

Well, this as I'm going to tell you only happened a few weeks ago, 'cos we haven't had ower water closet long. You see, my old uncle who lives over in Alderley lost his missus, so we asked him if he'd like to come over and stay with us for a week or so. He'd bin over before, but not since ower new water closet was set up just outside the back door. When we first had it my missus asked the farmer's wife what 'er should clean it with, not being used to having to do that, you see. The farmer's wife said, 'Well, if you haven't got any special lavatory cleaner, just pour some paraffin oil down the pan, that'll clean it.'

A propped-up privy in Canada, still used by the gardener

So, with my uncle a-comin' and 'er wanting it all to look nice and clean, 'er done just that and poured a good lot of paraffin down the lavatory, just before my old uncle Charley arrived.

Course, the first thing he wanted to do was to go to the privy, and went to go off down the garden. We stopped him, and said that we had got one nearer to the house now.

'Well', he said, 'I'll use 'im then, that'll save I a walk.'

So in he went and, as usual, straight away lit his old pipe – old men always smoked thur pipe in them places – and dropped the match in the pan. Suddenly, thur was the biggest bang as you ever heard, and out comes my old Uncle Charley with his trousers down round his ankles, braces dangling along the ground, and walking very funny-like.

'Bugger me,' 'e ses, 'thas the last time I etts pickled onions for breakfast.' Oh, we did laugh.

Another old fellow told me:

We had one a they vault privies, right away from the cottage. One night my mother went down there last thing, pitch-black it was, so it was up with her clothes as soon as her set foot in the privy, turned round and sat down.

We heard a-hollering and shouting, and rushed down there with a lantern. There was our mother shouting to a funny old man. What had happened was her had set down on an old tramp's lap, who was sleeping in there for the night.

In the mid 1930s, friends of mine were allowed to use a large twenty-plus roomed farmhouse (in Suffolk), until their new house was completed. The owner was in his seventies and the youngest of fourteen children. When asked about the emptying of the privy, he said that it had *never* been emptied. It was at the end of a long corridor in a large dark room; it was a three-seater, with a small one in the corner. My friend tried to find out the depth, but was unable to do so as it was full of bats. One night, rather than go there, he slipped into the garden and, in the dark, fell head first over an old sow.

And this happened a few years ago in Rhos, a Welsh village. There was this family privy of the usual three holes, with the biggest in the centre. A visitor, unaware of such seats, was missing for a long time, until the man of the house went to investigate, and found the visitor had put his two legs into the two outside holes and sat down on the middle one, and was stuck fast, unable to get out. Not a pretty sight!

From Tip Tree, near Colchester, comes this story:

My daughter was only three years old and although we didn't have a cat, she adored animals, and one day came into the garden with a white kitten from the farm, which they had 'lent' to her. She trotted off down the path with it and, unseen by me, went into the privy. Suddenly I heard cries of distress – she had put the kitten on the seat beside her and it had fallen down the big hole! We had a really *terrible* job getting the poor little thing clean! It was a real earth closet, not the bucket kind.

And one came from Mrs Bolton of Burnley:

When I was on a camping holiday in Wales, a farmer let me pitch my tent in his field. I asked him if I could use his loo, and was told that it was at the end of a path close to the house.

I couldn't believe my eyes as I opened the door to find the farmer's wife sitting on one hole of a three-seater loo, doing her job, and got even more of a shock when she called 'Come in'!

I did a quick about-turn, I can tell you.

Of course, city folk, at least during this century, didn't know much about earth privies. There was this young man, who had lived in London all his life and was used to water lavatories. Well, he went 'up north' to visit an old uncle who lived in rather a remote hamlet. The young man eventually asked where the lavatory was.

'There 'tis,' his uncle said, pointing to a wooden building down at the bottom of the garden.

When the young man returned to the cottage he said to his

At the end of the garden path . . .

uncle, 'That's a funny water system you got there. When I pulled the rope above the lav, no water came out.'

'We got no water down there,' his uncle roared, 'It's an earth closet, you bloody fool – you've let the pigeons out.'

This delightful story was told to me by a friend of mine, but she couldn't remember where she heard it:

The 'dunneck', as Jack called the lavatory, was down at the end of the garden path, and was built back-to-back and all under one roof with that of the cottage next door. The cross-members of timber that carried the wooden, boxed-in seats, were all in one piece and passed through the dividing wall. Over the years they had worked a little loose so that when you sat down the seats went up and down like a see-saw.

When Jack was in residence, he said he could always tell who was in the next door one by their weight. He could manage to outweigh either of the two daughters, and by sitting heavily and using all his weight he could even manage to keep the old lady up in the air, but when the master of the house paid a visit, Jack lost his supremacy, and his seat was suddenly elevated by about two inches. Then, he said that you had to be careful how you sat 'cos if the old man got up first you could do yourself a terrible mischief when the seat dropped down again sharpish.

And at a Women's Institute meeting in a village in the Forest

of Dean area, one of the members came up and told me this tale,
which she said had truly happened:

A soldier had returned from the second world war to find
that the old earth privy at his home was still being used. He
was all for building a lean-to nearer the house, and
suggested that they should have an Elsan which would be an
improvement on the old earth closet down the garden. This
they did, but his father still liked to use the old one. So the
soldier thought he'd soon make him change his mind, and
watched for the old fellow to 'pay a visit'. He got a hand-
grenade that he had brought home, he took out the pin and
aimed it near – not directly at – the old privy, the roof of
which promptly blew off. Out came the old fellow, trousers
around his ankles, and said, 'Good job I didn't let that fart
awf indoors.'

A lady evacuee from London was enquiring about a
furnished cottage, one in a row of six, that was to be let in a
Cotswold village. She looked round, and then said to the
owner, 'There's no privacy around here, is there?' The
owner replied, 'Oh, yes, there is, that's it, that little stone
place down the bottom of the garden. You share it with
your next-door neighbour.'

This following tale, given to me amongst many other 'privy' gems by Mrs Opie, was written by D.H. Richards:

All lavatories in the old days in the Black Country were 'open' or earth closets, usually at the bottom of the garden or at the top of a party yard and emptied every three months or so by the 'night soil' men who started their work when other folk were going to bed. When I was a child before the first world war, I have woken up scared to death with seeing the glare of flames on the ceiling and hearing the clanking of their buckets and their rough voices as they were busy emptying our closet at about two or three o'clock in the morning. They used to carry big paraffin flares of the kind they now place on corners and traffic islands in dense fog, and you could always tell when they had been because the seat, the floor and the paths would be covered with pink carbolic powder.

Those whose privies were in open yards or gardens with a back entrance were lucky, for the night soil men could come and go unnoticed. But if you lived in a row of houses as most people did, access to the rear was probably via an entry or veranda, and I might tell you that these places needed swilling next morning! These privies would become really foul smelling with the gas generated and many a time I've set fire to a piece of paper and dropped it into the pit just to see the vivid green and blue flames darting about as they ignited. I remember, at the bottom of Prince's End, three connected privies shared by about forty people, and

Out in the fields

once when the big common catch-pit was full, some
children dropped in a lighted paper and, as they hung over
the holes to see the little bright flames, a large volume of
gas ignited with a bang and the children, boys and girls, lost
eyelashes, eyebrows and front hair. Folks couldn't help
laughing at 'em. They did look funny.

This story came from Mrs L. Bentley of Headington, Oxford:

64

I remember vividly how, sixty years ago, with terrified caution I left the comfortable lamp-lit room for that dark little house at the bottom of the garden, opened the creaking door and thankfully sat over the hole of that well-scrubbed wooden seat. I was safe. Then my poor bare bottom was viciously attacked. My shrieks and the fluttering and squawking brought my parents running to meet me and rescue me from God knew what.

We ate the monster for our dinner the following day. Well, what would you have done to a cockerel that dared to get in through that little trap door at the back and roost on the bucket?

In a letter from Kings Sutton, near Banbury, comes this little tale:

I was born and brought up with me three brothers and sister at the village bakery, and we had a live-in mother's help called Iris. She was a distant relation of my father's, and always called him Uncle Perce and my mother Aunt May.

One winter's night when I was about six, I wanted 'to go', before bed time. So Iris took me up the garden path by the barn, which always seemed very spooky at night, to the privy which was between the barn and the pig sties. The candle would not stay alight because of the wind. Anyhow, Iris sent me in, in the dark, saying she would keep watch outside. I went to sit on the seat, felt 'something' and then there was a horrible raucous squawk, and a terrifying flapping of wings, and out flew the old white cockerel who had decided to roost there for the night. I cried. Iris shrieked and ran off, leaving me behind, and shouting for Uncle Perce to 'come quick there's a ghost in the lavatory'.

As long as Iris lived she never forgot this incident and told it over and over again – always with a laugh against herself.

CRASH IN LOO!

An oak tree felled by a gale collapsed onto an outside loo at West Chiltington, Sussex, while 73-year-old Jack Arnell was sitting inside. He said, 'I used to like peace and quiet there.'

This was told me by the late Chris Gittins, who played Walter Gabriel in *The Archers:*

The World Scout Jamboree was held at Sutton Park, Birmingham, on Bank Holiday 1957, to celebrate fifty years of scouting. Scouts from all nations were there. Since my teens I've been connected with the scout movement, so was very proud to be there.

Our latrines consisted of a great deep trench over which was fixed a long board with holes in, and each 'hole' was curtained off from the next with hessian. We found that the Red Indian scouts were very particular and refused to sit on the holes that everyone else was using. So they stood up or squatted on the seats.

Unfortunately that weekend the spirits of their ancestors must have inspired the rain god: the heavens opened and it tipped down with rain all day. You can imagine what a muddy state those seats got into: we had to hose them down continually before we could *sit* down.

T'ahtside closet

(A lovely little story to test your understanding of the Yorkshire dialect.)

Ahr ahtside closet were dahn at t'bottom o' t'gardin, an ah remember it well. What ah'm abaht ter tell yer 'appened when ah wer abaht ten year owd. T'Council chaps ed cum ter empty closet an' ah stood theer watchin' 'em. Ah thowt, by gum, theease chaps eve owd mucky job, an' es ah stood theer ah 'appened ter lewk up thru t'back doar an' saw t'rahnd 'oil 'at wi sat on, an' all on a sudden it struck mi. Mi aunt Penina ed clahted mi lug 'oil t'neet afore fer chasin' one o' 'er ducks ranhd t'backyard wi' a stick o' rhubarb. Soa ah thowt reight, this is it, t'next tahm mi aunt Penina goas ter t'closet ah'll wait 'till shoos getten on t'seat, then ah'll oppen t'back doar reight quiet like an' slap 'er backside wi' a stick

Like the old tin bath outside, this privy at Northmoor in Oxfordshire has seen better days

o'rhubarb, an' shood nivver knaw what 'ed 'it 'er. That way
ah'd get mi own back fer what soo'd dun ter mi. Onyrood
ah knew 'at t'vicar an' 'is wife were cumin' ter visit Aunt
Penina after t'service o' Sunda', soa ah laid mi plans well.
On t'Sunda' mornin' ah put two sticks o' rhubarb i' t'long
grass near t'closet doar, then went abaht mi bisness. That
neet ah positioned missen at t'back o' t'hen 'oil an' waited. It
wern't long afore ah saw aunt Penina traipsin' across t'yard
ter t'closet. Mi eyes leeted up, this wer it, nah fer it! Ah
gave 'er tahm ter get settled dahn, then crept up ter t'back
doar o' t'closet, oppened it, and lewked up, an' theer it wer,
all nicely framed an' ready fer t'smack o' a lahf tahm. Ah
picked up a stick o' rhubarb an' trahd a quiet swing fer
length, bura fun aht 'ah cudn't reich 'er backside wi'aht
'evvin ter step on t'midden flooar. Mi brain starts ter buzz,
then ah thowt that's it, that's answer, t'owd cloas prop. So
ah flew rahnd t'front o't'house fer ahr prop which ah knew
wer leanin' agin' t'fallpipe, grabbed it, an' es ah wer goin'
back ah thowt at t'midden doar wer pushed to, so ah pulled
it oppen an'lewked up ter make suer shoo wer still theer.
Shoo wer, so ah set missen, grippin' prop wi' all mi might
an' browt it up sharp, reight on 'er backside. Ah've nivver
'eeard a screeam lahk it ivve. Ah slammed doar shut an'
belted ranhd ter t'front o' t'house, put prop back ageean
t'fallpipe an' hid. Abaht arf an 'our later mi aunt Penina,
along wi't'vicar an' 'is wife, walked across t' yard. Ah lewked
at mi aunt fer signs o'damage, but shoo wer walking es
though now't 'ed 'appened. Ah cudn't fathom it aht 'es ah'd

gi'en 'er a real claht wi t'prop. Shoo said good neet ter t'vicar an' 'is wife, then went back in ter t'house. An' ah just stood theer flabbergasted. Theer went t'vicar an' 'is wife, poor divvel, 'owdin 'er backside wi' 'er reight 'and an' limpin'. Ther wer a long tahm afore they visited aunt Penina ageean, an' longer still afore they used 'er closet.

Finally, the ultimate danger! This story was told to me by a newspaper reporter, who swore that it was true:

Just before the last war broke out a young fellow of about eighteen was going to Austria to visit a relative. He was travelling by rail which would mean several days on the train. His mother, being a bit concerned about the hygiene of the train, said to him, 'I've packed you some newspapers, there will be so many people using the lavatories and they will get in a terrible state, so every time you sit on one lay a fresh piece of newspaper over the seat.'

As they got further into the Continent, quite often German soldiers would board the train, and at random pick out a few of the passengers and search them. One day, the young fellow was picked out and made to stand in the corridor while the soldiers searched him. The troops were quite ruthless, and suddenly one of them shouted 'strip', pointing a gun at him. Standing there, stark naked, they poked and pried. Suddenly one of them cried out in broken English, 'Look! Look! A spy!', to the others. They jabbered away, and then commanded the train to stop at the next station.

The author in Malta: 'I think I've just found a privy!'

The young man was kept under armed guard while the soldiers went further up the train. As the train pulled up, he was forced on to the platform and bundled into an army vehicle, then driven off at speed, still naked, shivering and shaking with cold and fright. When they finally reached an army camp, the young fellow was marched into a room where high-ranking officers were strutting about like so many peacocks. The officer-in-charge of the train raiding party explained why this young man had been brought there. He was ordered to bend down while they all examined his backside, words like 'spy', 'secret code' and 'maps' were shouted in broken English. 'What have you to say?' one of the officers commanded.

By now the lad had realized what had happened: when he had last laid some newspaper on the very wet lavatory seat, some of it must have stuck to his backside. This he explained. A mirror was found, and shame-facedly the officer-in-charge was told to read out what he could make of it: it happened to be part of page six of a three-week-old *Sunday Times*.

A Secret Place

Some privies have been found in curious places – and some curious things have been found in privies!

At Oriel College, Oxford, in 1982, a seventeenth-century privy was discovered when an old fireplace was demolished, first revealing an underground chamber. Experts from the Oxford Archaeological Society were called in. It was not built as a lavatory in the first place, but was used to store the College silver during the Civil War. Then it was used as a loo by Robert Say, the Provost of Oriel, and his wife and family, who lived in part of the College. When the piles of chocolate-brown material were analysed, it was found that the Provost and his family had apparently lived on a rich diet of fruit – for seeds and stones of *all* types of English fruit – cherries, wild strawberries, raspberries, plums, gooseberries and mulberries – were found along with the seeds of figs and grapes and other exotic foods. Also found down

Loo at the Bishop of Winchester's Palace, Witney. Nigel Swietalsky excavates an early thirteenth-century pot (Oxford Archaeological Unit)

there were a number of clay pipes: it's assumed the Provost smoked in there, probably to take away the smell as there was no kind of ventilation for the cess pit.

In *Alfriston, a Sussex Village* (1970) Rex A. Marchant refers to 'Mrs Washer, who died in 1771. Nearly £1200 was found hidden about her house, including over £100 in "the necessary house".'

In my part of the world, at Witney in Oxfordshire, evidence has recently come to light that the nobility was well set up with sanitary arrangements as early as the twelfth century. In 1984, a firm of builders were working in the grounds of Mount House, with the idea of building several flats there, when they came across the remains of the Bishop of Winchester's Palace that had once stood on the site. It was first built in 1110, but was transformed in 1129 by Henry of Bloss, Bishop of Winchester, and, among other improvements made at that time were the up-to-date lavatories described as 'the most spectacular domestic latrines in Norman England'.

I am glad that at last people are realizing that the privies are precious and ought to be treasured. Not so long ago the Department of the Environment astonished Mr Ernie Smith, a farmer, by declaring his run-down three-seater outside family lavatory at Bishop's Tawton, North Devon, a listed building. It has not been used for more than thirty years and is covered in brambles.

UNEARTHING MEDIEVAL SECRETS OF THE CLOSET
by David Keys

Archaeologists in Winchester, Hampshire, have unearthed 16 cubic feet of human excrement, appropriately located beneath a toilet seat made in about 1300.

Every cubic inch promises to provide scientists with fascinating details of what the medieval lavatory-users were eating – and the stomach parasites from which they suffered.

The excrement probably emanated from people who occupied the former residence of one of England's wealthiest merchants, a wool magnate and local MP named John De Tyntnge, who died in 1312.

The district in which the house was located went down-market when Winchester ceased to be England's leading wool-trading centre outside London.

The house, which probably had twelve rooms, was built in the thirteenth century and was demolished in 1370. Archaeological excavations have revealed the complete ground floor layout of the building – lavatory included.

The excavation is being financed by Winchester City Council and Cultural Resources Management, which runs the highly successful Yorvik Viking Centre in York. The Winchester dig, and an accompanying exhibition, is open to the public.

The Independent
15 August 1987

One day I was signing books in a local shop when a woman came in and told me this story:

Relations of hers had recently bought a delightful Cotswold stone farmhouse just outside Burford. One of the first things they asked the builders to do was to pull out the pre-war fireplace – an architect friend had told them that behind it there would be an old open fireplace. Sure enough, there it was with a great oak beam over the top, and an inglenook seat either side. Then the builders noticed a big iron key hung up in the inglenook, and they began to chat with the

Two-holer still in use in the village of Leighterton

owner to try and find out why it was there and which door
it was supposed to unlock. Then the labourer, an old fellow
of about seventy, came in. Did he know what it was for?

'Ah,' the old man said to the owner, 'You got an old privy
right down the yard, 'ent you?'

'Yes,' she replied.

'Well, give us the key, I reckon I knaws where 'e fits.'

Sure enough, it was the key to the old privy.

'But why hang it on there?' asked the owner.

'Well,' the old fellow replied, 'Like as not thur was a big
family living yer at one time, so they had to work out an
arrangement. If the key wur hung up in the inglenook, then

thur was nobody in the privy. Likewise, if the key wur missing, then the place was occupied. 'Twas a simple as that.'

And my old friend, Harold Greening from Winchcombe, told me this story about someone else who hid things in the privy:

Before my great uncle Fred walked to Wales to find work, at the beginning of the 'coal rush', he lived and worked in Winchcombe. His favourite pub was the White Lion which was quite near his home in Ale Street, near the old silk mill. He was quite a cunning fellow and always on the look-out for something to nick.

One night, as usual, he went for his half pint at the White Lion, but at closing time, instead of going home he set off out of Winchcombe, right up the hill towards Bella's Knap, a prehistoric burial mound. Just beyond there lay Wontley Farm. A few days before that, in an open shed, Fred had noticed there were signs that at night some hens were roosting in there. He made for the shed, quietly and quickly he killed and stuffed half a dozen hens in a sack bag and made off for home. Keeping to the back roads and lanes, at last he came to the lane near the silk mill.

Before going indoors he went down the garden to the old privy and carefully hung the sack of hens on a hook under the privy seat: it had been emptied recently so the sack hung clear of the contents. Then he went indoors, kicked off his boots and sprawled himself in front of the lovely fire.

Soon his face was red with the heat, and the fact that he had come in from the cold wind.

He hadn't bin sat there long when there was a knock on the door, and his wife answered it. 'Twas the village constable!

'Where's Fred?' he asked.

'Sitting by the fire, constable, why don't you come in out of the cold and join him'.

After he'd sat down the constable said, 'Wur you bin tonight, then, Fred?'

'Down to the Lion, 'ad me half a pint, why?'

'Well', said the officer, 'I saw somebody skulking about around the back lane, but missed him somehow. I thought perhaps it was you.' 'But,' he went on, 'I can see taint you I wants, so I'll wish you both goodnight.'

Years later Fred came back to Winchcombe to live, and having heard the story many times, Mr Greening, his great-nephew, asked him what he did with the hens.

'Ett um, of course, they were alright after they'd bin 'feathered. 'Course, as soon as I thought the copper was gone home, I went down to the old privy and fetched 'um up home.'

From the book *The Crisis of the Aristocracy, 1558–1641*, by Lawrence Stone comes the following:

Medical objections to a heavy diet were complemented by the disapproval of the moralists, who regarded an over-

loaded table as a scandalous waste of money. The futility of
thus stimulating the digestive cycle was proverbial, 'a great
housekeeper is sure of nothinge for his good cheare save a
great Turd at his gate', was the elegant aphorism of the
yokels of Gloucestershire. But few of the nobility and
greater gentry heeded the warning, and more than one of
them could be said to have 'sent all his revenues downe the
privy house'.

And here is another tale of revenues that ended up in the
privy:

The relations of old Willum King knew that the old fellow
had a bit of money put by, but when he died nobody could
find any. Yet when he was alive he used to show folk his
collection of sovereigns – ah! he'd got about two dozen of
them and quite a few half sovereigns as well. He kept them
in a very small leather bag tied with a thong, and he always
carried it with him.

Well, after Willum's funeral his relations almost pulled
the cottage apart, but it was no use, the hoard of sovereigns
couldn't be found, and in the end they gave it up as a bad
job.

And the cottage where Willum and his forefathers had
lived was left to fall into ruin. Over the years villagers
carried away some of the stone for walls and rockeries, and
the once lovely garden became a wilderness.

Many years later, when building land was fetching a good

price, the cottage – what was left of it – was sold. Willum's only living relative, a great niece, was only too glad to see the back of it.

When the builders were taking down what was left of the old privy, they found the rotted remains of a little leather bag, still hung on a nail, under the seat.

'Wonder what the hell that was hung in there for?' remarked one chap, as they shovelled what had been the contents of the old privy on to a lorry ready to be taken away to the local dump.

A very discreet privy, astride a stream

A Miscellany

of Lavatorial Items

Privies have given rise to some strange scenes and some strange ideas. Here's just a few of them, the first from a Mr Penny:

I well remember my late father (who came from the village of Aldbourne, Wiltshire), telling me that on leaving the village school he was apprenticed as a carpenter locally. He was taken one day to a remote cottage to assist an older carpenter in making and fitting a new wooden seat to the existing outside privy. The elderly woman occupant of the cottage was very noisy and kept interfering and getting in the way. The old carpenter decided to have a bit of fun with her, and having made the new wooden seat and put it in place, he called the woman out to the privy and asked her to sit down on it. She asked why. The carpenter told her that as he had to cut out the hole in the privy top he needed her to sit on it so that he could mark around her backside in order to get the hole the right size!

That got rid of her – she shot off like a scalded cat!

It seems that, probably to relieve the tensions of war, servicemen in particular seemed to have derived a great delight in 'warming up' their mates while they were sitting on the communal latrines. Most, it seems, were built in a row, with a channel of continuous running water serving the row of privies. The standing joke was to drop a piece of rag, well soaked in petrol, which could be lighted at the top end, the flowing water would gradually take it down the row causing pain and surprise to those sitting on those holes. One man who experienced this, said: 'I was at the top end, so it wasn't too bad, but them bottom ones copped it. Their privates was singed of hair as bare as a yew stick.'

This lovely memory came from a lady who lives at Shabbington, Aylesbury:

I was born in a thatched cottage at Draycott, on the road from Ickford to Tiddington in Oxfordshire. We had a privy at the bottom of the garden and my sister and I used to cut newspaper in squares, which we all used in there: it was the only means we had – no such thing as 'toilet paper' in those days. At that time my uncle and aunt were in service at Waddesdon Manor, in Buckinghamshire, home of the Rothschilds. My uncle was head groom and my aunt cooked for all the staff who worked in the gardens.

PRIVIES GALORE

Miss Rothschild used to give my aunt books that she had finished with – the *Tatler*, and things like that. My aunt passed them on to my mother when we called to see them. The magazines were not much good as 'bum fodder', much too stiff and shiny for that, you see. So my mother used to leave them in the privy for my dad to look at when he paid a visit down there. In those days, most everybody used to read in their lavatories.

One day I was sitting on the privy and thought I'd take a look at the magazines, and out of one fell two one-pound notes!

Very excitedly I ran back to our cottage, my knickers half-up, half-down. My mother thought it was a fortune – it was more money than my father earned in two weeks. The only thing we could think was that Miss Rothschild used the £1 notes as *bookmarks*.

When my dad came home we told him, and he ran down to the old privy and went through every page of those magazines, but he didn't find any more.

Did you know that George II died on the throne – literally?

He was in his closet when his valet, hearing 'a noise louder than the Royal Wind', rushed in to find that Death had levelled the king flat on his face on the floor of his loo.

This extract was sent to me from America:

The art world is buggy over a newly discovered painting by William de Kooning (of the Long Island de Koonings). A breathless agent has announced that the price is beyond estimate. This is because the taste of art fanciers is only more mysterious than the source of their wealth.

It is a fairly simple painting on a long rectangle of poplar wood (the very material, by the way, upon which the Mona Lisa is painted), broken by three carved voids in the shape of asymmetrical ovals. The borders of the ovals are carefully smoothed and burnished with the sort of patina one usually sees on the toes of the statues of saints, where the true believers have rubbed the statue for good luck.

Anyone over forty who has ever spent time in a rural environment, or a poorly appointed summer camp, would recognise the object for what it is, and what it is, is: a three-holer.

This is not the first painted three-holer which your correspondent has ever seen, although it is true that most of these objects (and by far the largest number of them are more modest, or less sociable, one-and-two-holers) are made of unpainted wood.

Mr de Kooning's contribution (the sculptor is unknown) is unfortunately rather trivial, although perhaps intended to be humorous. He has simply, sometime before World War II, applied white and black paint to the object with the apparent intention of making it look like marble, that is, to elevate it from a merely functional lower-class object to a spurious upper-class object which would be an appropriate adjunct to croquet parties. There are some unrepresentational splotches of black paint which the art authorities tell us are 'angry' in their tone, which may say something about Mr de Kooning's attitude towards the three-holers or which may say something about the sobriety of the painter at the time he was executing the commission. On the other hand, it may only say something about these art critics.

The painting is currently hung horizontally against a vertical wall, which somewhat tends to obscure its true nature, except, of course, to flies, who work equally well whether sitting on the wall or the ceiling, and therefore have no built-in preference as to whether they should look at a three-holer from head-on or overhead. Flies, on the other hand, have no aesthetic preferences either, and probably enjoyed the object more when it was in its previous incarnation.

M.R. Montgomery
The Boston Globe
21 January 1985

I've heard privy seats called some funny things in my time – but never art!

LOOS CHANGE

Stand-up toilets for women are being tried out in Pensacola, Florida, by a company whose woman boss finds conventional facilities inconvenient.

Daily Express
January 1988

August 24, 1736: A remarkable fat boar was seen coming out of the Fleet Street Ditch into the Thames. It proved to belong to a butcher near Smithfield Bars, who had missed the animal for five months. All the time, it seems, he had been in the *common sewer* and was improved in price from ten shillings to two guineas.

(From *Harrington's Metamorphosis*, by A.H.T. Robb-Smith)

One lady from Norway told me:

In my town some of the public lavatories – water ones – are operated by a foot pedal rather than a chain. But unfortunately many 'visitors' missed seeing the pedal. In one there is a large notice which says: 'Please to trample the treadle'.

And another, this time from Sweden, sent me this snippet:

A practical joker had a two-holer behind the gas station where he was working. Under the seat he had set up a loudspeaker, and whenever there was a young lady using the toilet, he would take the microphone in his office and say: 'Sorry, ma'am, would you mind using the other hole, we're working down here!'

From Queen's College, Oxford, comes this item of news. In the year 1374, John Wyclif, the church reformer, who at that time was known as 'The Morning Star of the Reformation', apparently had his own privy to which he held the key. Quite a privilege at that time as the other Fellows and students had to use a communal one.

And in 1987 there seemed to be a great interest in the Oxford Union Debating Chamber. The powers-that-be wanted to change the Gents' Victorian bathroom by lowering the ceiling, so that a 'Ladies' toilet could be built in the 'air space'.

Students said that if this was carried out it would ruin the bathroom's historical value: they pointed out that at least five Prime Ministers had peed in there – Gladstone, Asquith, Lloyd George, Macmillan and Heath had all at some time passed through the wooden door.

Mrs Rachell Hayes, of Birmingham Road, Redditch, discovered my interest in privies in unusual places and sent me some photographs of Abberley church clock tower. It was built in 1880, and right inside the tower is a privy – I wonder for whose benefit it was positioned in the church, the parson's or the congregation's?

Abberley church . . .

. . . and its inside privy

American outside WC

This tale was printed recently in a national newspaper:

Staff at a council old people's home decided to teach a thief a lesson after a bottle of whisky intended as a raffle prize was stolen. They filled a Scotch bottle with urine and left it in the same place – and now that has gone too!

Said Susan Dale, principal officer at Idsall Court, Shifnal, Shropshire, 'All we can say now to the thief is cheers – there's plenty more where that came from.'

Even members of the royal family show an interest in Victorian lavatories. A few years ago, when a part of Sandringham House was demolished, Queen Elizabeth asked that three nineteenth-century lavatories should be preserved for the royal family's curio collection.

And from a daily paper comes this account:

> When the royal couple chatted with a group of children, Fergie revealed her favourite feature of Windsor castle – the loos!
>
> Asked if living in a castle was primitive, she said: 'The great thing is the loos. They have great, old fashioned loos.
>
> 'They don't have any cistern or chain – you have to pull a chain up from the ground.
>
> 'Then all the water rushes down and they open up underneath.'

One day a man was on his rounds collecting rents on a Council Estate. Apparently in each building the back door to the houses and the one to the outside WC were side by side and quite close to one another. The rent collector, as usual, knocked, pushed open the door and called out.

'I've come for me dues, Mrs Jones,' he said, but had opened the wrong door, only to find Mrs Jones enthroned on her WC.

This is an excerpt from a letter from an American mother to her son, who was serving in Europe during World War II:

Pop has got a job, the first since before you were born.

What with that and your allowance, we decided to launch out a bit and build the bathroom we've always aimed for. It was finished a week ago. It's a swell job. In one corner is a large kind of tub, a bit bigger than the pig trough. That's for washing all over. On the same side as that is a smaller basin in which you can wash your face and hands. In the other corner is a pedestal arrangement for your feet. First you wash one in it and then you pull a chain and down comes a fresh supply of water for you to wash the other. And that's not all! The firm that sent out the fittings is generous. They sent a mahogany frame, though they forgot the glass, and we've put this up in the parlour with an enlargement of Grandpop's picture in it. They also sent a solid board that makes a swell bread board, and several rolls of writing paper . . .

Whether or not this is true, this vivid description is reproduced in the USA – on a greetings card!

This is quoted from an old Gloucester newspaper:

The town council of Cheltenham Spa voted to replace the words 'Men' and 'Women' on some of the public lavatories to 'Ladies' and 'Gentlemen' – in order to attract a better class of people.

I have received letters about privies from so many places. A nice one came from J.C. Liebe-Harkort of Sweden, who writes about privies he has known:

> Behind the big house of my grandparents, there used to be a two-holer (a child/grown-up one), that was used only in emergencies since there was a water closet in the house. This WC was installed at the end of the eighteenth century (of course, without water to begin with), and my parents tell me that the people in the small town used to say: *Dat sinn fine Lü, die hant Hüsken innert Huus!*, which is a form of German as atrocious and loveable as your Cotswold variety of English. It means: 'They are really posh people, they have the "little house" inside the house!'

He goes on,

> The biggest lavatory I've seen was an eight-holer that belonged to an amusement park in Mora in Dalekarlia. There was some sort of fur around the edge of the holes – quite cozy but not very hygienic, I'm afraid.
>
> I found a real beauty many years ago; it was standing high on a cliff on one of the 24,000 islands of the Stockholm Archipelago, and had a big window in the door which gave a fine view over the sea. In a corner inside was a chain with a porcelain knob hanging from the roof. Since human beings live by habits, no newcomer could ever resist pulling the chain. Naturally there was no flush of water (what you

had done went down the cliff edge); instead you got a mighty blast from a truck's horn and everybody would say 'Oh! he/she has finished'.

Ernst Toller, author of *I was a German* (1934) was President of the Central Committee. As soon as the Soviet Republic was declared in Bavaria, he was beseiged by cranks, who each had their own nostrum for the ills of humanity. This was in Munich, 1919:

Some believed that the root of all evil was cooked food, others the gold standard, others hygienic underwear, or machinery, or the lack of a compulsory universal language, or multiple stores, or birth control. They reminded me of the Swabian shoemaker who wrote a voluminous pamphlet to prove that man owed his mortal sickness to the fact that he satisfied his elementary needs in closed rooms with the aid of artificial paper; whereas if he spent these daily moments out in the woods and availed himself of the natural moss all spiritual poisons would also evaporate into the surrounding air; and he would be at the same time bodily and spiritually purified, returning to his work with a strengthened social conscience and a diminished egoism; true love of humanity would be awakened and the Kingdom of God on earth would be at hand.

From *A Doctor in The Forest* by Dr Bill Tandy comes this little gem:

It was about ten o'clock one November night when I got a telephone call to go and see Thomas Oliver. He lived up a very narrow lane a few miles away. When I got the message I groaned inwardly, not only was Thomas Oliver a bit of a cantankerous old man, but it was a *very* foggy night. I had great difficulty in finding the narrow lane along which Thomas lived and visability was about one yard. Carrying my bag in one hand and a torch in the other I groped my way up the lane. Then I saw a faint light shining dimly round the margins of a shut door. I opened the gate and soon arrived at the door. I knocked, no response, I knocked again more loudly. Then the door opened about an inch and a voice said, 'What d'yer want?'

'I've come to see Mr Oliver,' I replied.

''Im baint 'ere' came the reply. And the door was shut and the bolt drawn across. After my struggles to get to the house I found this reception more than a bit disconcerting, and again banged loudly on the door.

'I've come to see Mr Oliver,' I said again. The door opened about an inch.

''Im baint in 'ere, I'm tellin' yer,' and again the door was shut tight.

Again I hammered on the door; it opened very slightly. I said, 'If Mr Oliver isn't in, is Mrs Oliver in?'

''Er baint in, nobody baint in 'ere but me.'

An interestingly shaped building housing a one-holer, found in a deserted garden

'Look here,' I said, 'I'm the doctor, I've come all this way in the fog to see him, what is going on in this house?'

''Ouse' said the voice, 'this baint 'ouse, 'ouse is up garden path, this 'ere's the privy.'

Dobson masquerades as a gentleman and tells his school fellows, who are to act as serving-men, 'When I call or speake to you, forget not to stand with your heads uncovered, or if I stand to piffe, you must also stand bare at my backe, after an English fashion.'

(From *Dobsons Drie Bobbes: a story of sixteenth-century Durham*, ed. Horsman, 1607)

There were details of French manners, certainly, which displeased all the party – . . . a court lady's close-stool open beside her bed as the visitors were shown through, not to mention the crude behaviour of the lower orders in Paris, where 'the women sit down in the streets as composedly as if they were in a convenient-house with the doors shut'.

(*Samuel Johnson and His World*, Margaret Lane, 1975)

Traveling conveniences for army officers

A collector of period furniture was interested in an old chair:

'It's Queen Anne,' the salesman said.

'Oh, yes,' said the collector, 'how can you tell?'

'Well,' the salesman replied, 'look at the letters carved on it: Q.A. That stands for Queen Anne, surely.'

'If that stands for Queen Anne,' cried the collector, not impressed, 'I've got a door at home that dates back to William the Conqueror.'

In the early days of motoring, a man was out driving his car. He passed through a large village where there was a single petrol pump, but didn't stop as he thought that he had enough fuel in his tank to get home – a matter of about four miles. About a mile and a half along the road the car came to a halt, no petrol. So the driver looked around the car to see if he could find something to carry a drop of petrol – just enough to take him back to the petrol pump. All that he could find was a small enamelled potty which belonged to his little girl.

He arrived back at the car and was just pouring the petrol into his tank when another car pulled up. The driver, a vicar, poked his head out, and said, 'I don't know what your religion is, but I do admire your faith.'

The highly entrepreneurial and personable Lord Brocket is so enormously proud of his lavatories at Brocket Hall, Hertfordshire, that he has entered them in a Loo of the Year competition.

They are rather singular contraptions and, one imagines, a joy to use. 'They were originally the public toilets at Shepherd's Bush underground station,' said his lordship. 'We managed to get all the mahogany panels, doors, taps and marble tops as well as several glass cisterns.'

These were then converted so that Lord, and presumably Lady Brocket, can now gaze upon goldfish swimming about happily up above while they get on with their business.

Says the owner of these unique water closets: 'Men want a loo that reeks of class no matter what their background.'

Incidentally, fish fanciers might like to know that the goldfish are in no danger as a clever system of valves prevents them from being flushed away.

Daily Express

From Mr Foreman of Oxford came this piece of interesting information:

In a large privy which was part of the ruined Hampton Gay Manor, generations of visitors have left their graffiti there, and boldly scratched across one wall is this statement:

One would think by all this wit,
that Shakespeare had been here to —

And for the archives, or the privy walls, from Gloucestershire:

Oh what a blessing, as women can shit without undressing,
But we poor sons of bitches, must undress or shit our
breeches.

Graffiti on a lavatory wall in one of the Oxford colleges, written in Greek, translated to English, reads:

Everything passes
Nothing remains
Aristagoras

Someone had added:

Everything remains
Nothing passes
Constipagoras

I was very interested in this from a letter that was written, after he had read *Cotswold Privies*, by Mr S.C.B. Dealey, Senior, of Cheltenham, to his son who passed it on to me.

When I was a boy, nearly ninety years ago, earth closets were in universal use – we had one. I was surprised that the author did not mention the fact that the 'buckets' which superseded the earth closets were introduced – at least into Birmingham – by the Rt. Hon. Joseph Chamberlain, and were known as 'Chamberlain Pianos'.

When we moved from Smethwick to City Road, Birmingham, we had two WCs, one upstairs next to the bathroom, and one down in the yard. My mother would never use the indoor one, as she considered it 'unhealthy'. Your grandfather used to recite the following:

> In the great House of Commons
> The backbone of our land
> When a motion is made
> The member must stand
> But in this neat cottage privy
> Now don't on it frown
> When a motion is made
> The member sits down

Heard in my village was a mother shouting to her child who kept running in and out of the house, 'Fer goodness sake, be still for five minutes. You be in and out of here like a fart in a colander.'

And this tale I heard years ago from the girl who lived next door to this woman who, whilst in her privy way down her garden, was heard to shout to her husband:

'Garge, Garge, bring I a fork, quick.'

Garge goes rushing down and hands her a garden fork.

'Not that sort of fork, yu B—F—,' she shouted. 'I means a fork what you eats yer dinner with. I got a knot in the 'lastic of me knickers, and until I gets it undone I can't set down and have a good 'un.'

One elderly lady told me that when she and her six sisters were small, and the privy was a good walk away, their mother used to hold the baby over the coal bucket and let her do it in there.

'My word,' she added, 'that stunk summut awful when our mother made the fire up. Mind you,' she added, 'thur was a bigger stink when our dad and a neighbour who we shared the privy with, emptied it once a year. They got ninety buckets full of — out of it.'

And one of the vivid memories of my youth was when I went to Ducklington village school and the lavatories were of the bucket type, with a trap door at the back – for emptying purposes. Boys used to pick bunches of stinging nettles, wait until a girl went in, then they would open the trap door and shove the nettles in – stinging the unfortunate occupant on the backside. They did it to me once: I caught them and boxed their ears. They didn't try that hookham on me again!

This lovely story came from Mrs Delvoe from Bournemouth – she had just read an article about me and my privies in a magazine, and wondered if this story would interest me. I must admit I've never heard anything like it before. She writes:

An English lady was to stay in a small German village. Not knowing any German she secured the help of a German schoolmaster, and wrote to him for information. One of her questions was to ask, was there a WC attached to her lodgings? The schoolmaster, not familiar with the abbreviation, thought that WC might mean Wold Chapel – which means 'Chapel in the Woods'. Thinking that she must be a devout Church-goer, he wrote her the following letter:

> The WC is situated some seven miles from your lodgings, in the midst of beautiful scenery, and is open Tuesdays, Thursdays, Fridays and Sundays. This is unfortunate if you are in the habit of going frequently, but you will be interested to know that some people take their lunch with them, and make a day of it, whilst others go by car and arrive just in time.
>
> As there are many visitors in the summer, I do advise you to go early. The accommodation is good, and there are about 60 seats, but if at any time you should be late arriving, there is plenty of standing room. The bell is rung 10 minutes before the WC is open. I advise you to visit on a Friday as there is an organ recital on that day.
>
> I should be delighted to secure a seat for you and be the first to take you there. My wife and I have not been for six months, and it pains us very much – but it is a long way to go.
>
> Hoping this information will be of some use to you.
>
> Yours sincerely . . .

A Privy

By Any Other Name

It's amazing how many different names folk can think up for a privy or for 'powdering their nose'. I've included all the ones I've collected here – but I'm sure there are lots more.

A 'certain' place
Asterroom
Biffy
Bombay
Chamber of Commerce
Chamberlain pianos ('bucket lav')
Chuggie
Crapphouse
Crapping Castle
Dike
Dinkum-dunnies

Doneks
Dubs
Duffs
Go and have a Jimmy Riddle
God and have a Tim Tit
Going to pick daisies
Going to see a man about a dog
Going to stack the tools
Going to the George
Going to the groves
Gone where the wind is always
   blowing
Here is are
Holy of Holies
Honk
House of Commons
House of Office
Jericho
Larties
Latrine

My Aunts
Petty
Place of repose
Place of retirement
Round-the-back
Shunkie
The Backhouse
The Boggy a the bottom
The Bush
The Convenience
The Dispensary
The Dunny
The End
The Grot
The Halting Station
The Hoojy-boo (attributed to Dame
    Edith Evans)
The house where the Emperor goes
    on foot
The Hum
The Jakers

The Jampot
The Japping
The John
The Lats
The Long drop
The Offices
The Opportunity
The Ping-pong house
The Proverbial
The Sammy
The Shants
The Shot-Tower
The Sit house
The Small house
The Tandem (a two-holer)
The Watteries
The Wee house
The Whatjucallit
Widdlehouse
Windsor Castle
'Yer Tiz'

Especially for WCs:

Adam & Eve
Chain of Events
Flushes and Blushes
The Penny House
The Plumbing

The Porcelain Pony
The Water Box
UMTAG (USSR version of WC)
Going to inspect the plumbing
The urinal

One definition of a privy which I have had suggested to me is that it is, 'that place where men of studious minds are apt to sit longer than the ordinary fellow'.

One of the perennial debates in our newspapers and over the dinner table is the origin of the word 'loo'. One early contender has already appeared on page 53, and here is a selection of other correspondence on the issue. Mrs Opie supplied me with one definition she took from a newspaper in 1967:

A promising candidate for the origin of 'loo' for lavatory is the French *lieux d'aisances*, which means the place itself, a privy, without any traditional meaning.

ORIGIN OF 'LOO'

Sir – Cdr. A. Dunhill's ingenious explanation of the possible origin of the word 'loo' (Aug. 31), is interesting, but surely there is an alternative and much simpler possibility: namely that the word is derived from 'ablution'.

Yours faithfully,
(Dr) G.H. Lewis
Harlow, Essex.

'Luliana'

Sir – Prof. Alan Ross may be interested to know that the word 'loo' is derived from '*luliana*,' which was in use 50 years ago.

Yours faithfully,
PHILIP CARPENTER
Estartit, Spain.

Daily Telegraph
13 September 1968

This correspondence had been going on for some time.

Caption to cartoon by du Maurier:

Curate: 'Now we'll begin again at the Hallelujah, and please linger longer on the "lu!" '

Punch

22 June 1895

This is another definition which was offered to Mrs Opie:

In case you ask about the word 'loo' (privy). To those working in the country, natural functions were often performed in the open in the shelter of a hedge, copse, wood, etc., in the loo (lee) i.e., out of the wind. The 'privies' attached to isolated cottages and farms were at the end of the garden or yard, often with no door, or sometimes under a tree, but one was out of the wind, i.e., in the loo. The old time navvy always put his up in a sheltered place if possible, with its back to the wind so that when nature called, he could have a smoke in the loo. As boys we often smoked elm root in the 'loo' of a hedge or hut.

This letter from the historian Sir Steven Runciman to Lord Lichfield, the photographer, is quoted in Frank Muir's *A Book at Bathtime* (Heinemann). It is, we are assured, the one *true* origin of the word 'loo', and in his letter Sir Steven says 'it was told me by the Duke of Buccleuch's aunt, Lady Constance Cairns. Your relations feature largely in it.'

In 1867 (Lady Constance was not absolutely certain of the date), when the first Duke of Abercorn was Viceroy of

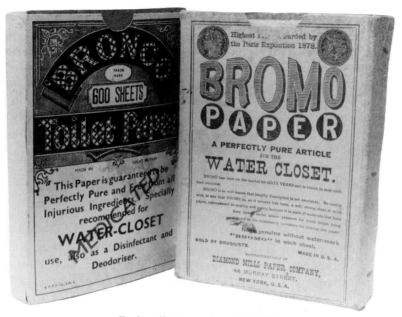

Early toilet paper from the USA

Ireland, there was a large house-party at the Viceregal
Lodge, and among the guests there was the Lord
Lieutenant of the County Roscommon, Mr Edward King
Tennyson, and his wife, Lady Louisa, daughter of the Earl
of Lichfield.

Lady Louisa was, it seems, not very loveable; and the
two youngest Abercorn sons, Lord Frederick and Lord
Ernest, took her name-card from her bedroom door and
placed it on the door of the only WC in the guest wing. So,
in those select ducal circles everyone talked of going to Lady
Louisa.

Then people became more familiar – Jimmy Abercorn
[the present duke] told me that when he was a boy one
went to 'Lady Lou' (though he had never been told who her
ladyship was).

Now, in these democratic days the courtesy title has been
dropped, and within the last 30 years or so – only really
since the war – the term has seeped down into middle-class
and even working-class usage. But it all really originated
with your Hamilton uncles being ungallant to your Anson
aunt; who, I think should have her immortality recognised.

Privy Poets

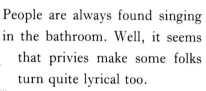

People are always found singing in the bathroom. Well, it seems that privies make some folks turn quite lyrical too.

One day I was visiting Chipping Campden and got talking to an elderly man and the subject somehow got round to privies. He told me that the lads of the town used to sing a ditty to the tune of 'Sweet Violets' when the lavendar cart went by:

My father was a midnight mechanic
He worked at the middens all night
And when he came home in the morning
He was covered all over in . . .

The author enjoying a 'slipper bath'

Sweet violets, sweeter than all the roses
Covered all over from head to foot,
Covered all over in . . . Sweet violets.

He worked with a scoop and a shovel,
With only a candle to light
And without 'ere a word or a warning
Down tumbled six bucks of . . .

Sweet violets . . .

Marcus Binney, writing in *Country Life* in January 1985, about a great collection of stool-type conveniences amassed by Carl Gustav Wrangel in the seventeenth century, reported that one of them had a nice piece of verse inscribed on it:

> Though your name be Modesty
> Sweetly budding rose
> Needs must when you enter here
> Your private parts expose

There's an epigraph on a tombstone to an old woman buried somewhere in Gloucestershire – well, so an old Gloster-man told me – that reads so:

> Where ever you be
> Let the wind go free
> For the queeze of a fart
> Was the death of me

Anyhow, that would not have been good advice for the following:

According to the ancient Laws of Manu, every conceivable part of the body was liable to be amputated as a punishment, including the anus, of any citizen who might break wind in front of the king.

> (Guido Manjno, *The Healing Hand:*
> *Man and Wound in the Ancient World*)

An old fellow in my village was asked why he spent such a long time in the privy. His reply was:

> Well, sometimes I just sets and thinks
> And sometimes I just sets and stinks
> Other times I just sets

And this was scribbled on the wall of a friend's privy:

> This is not a place
> To sit and slumber
> But piddle and shit
> And fart like thunder.
> Have done with windy argument and let the matter drop.

This poem comes from a military magazine of *c*. 1941:

Retreats

Soldiers, please pause while I tell you two laws,
Of the rears which should cause no surprise.
The first of the two is called cover from view,
And the second is cover from flies,
When you've done what you can in the tin or the pan,
Don't think it a terrible bore,

To sprinkle some sand on the top with your hand,
From a box you will find on the floor
If there should be a dearth of this so-called dry earth,
Your plan is quite easy to see,
You conceal what you pass with a few blades of grass,
Or a leaf from a neighbouring tree.
For flies do with ease spread a lot of disease,
So from this it is perfectly clear,
Conceal your excreta, it looks so much neater,
And keeps flies away from the rear.

Notice in a two-seater at Beck Row, Mildenhall, Suffolk:

If you wish to keep this temple sweet
Open the door and shut down the seat

'*To Symon Gray*' was written by Burns on his Border tour, when Symon Gray, who lived near Duns, sent him a copy of verses for his inspection:

Such damn'd bombast no age that's past
  Can show, nor time to come;
So, Symon dear, your song I'll tear,
  And with it wipe my bum.

The anonymous author of this verse offers a nice comment on the privy:

> Snug in an English garden's shadiest spot
> A structure stands, and welcomes many a breeze
> Lonely and simple as the ploughman's cot
> Where monarchs may unbend who wish for ease

And Mrs Joyce Latham of Coleford in the Forest of Dean has dedicated her skills to the privy, in the following ode:

Down the garden path

> Coust thee remember, owd 'un, when we all had WCs
> Away down in the gyarden where we used to take our ease?
> 'Twere like a little palace wi' some matting on the floor,
> Thic seat were scrubbed as white as snow, and hung
> behind the door
> Upon a large and sturdy nail, in pieces cut to size,
> All threaded on a piece of string, unheeding of the flies.
> Thee't vind a yup o' newspaper – its purpose plain to see,
> In them days proper toilet rolls seemed awful posh to me.
> Carbolic and Jeyes Fluid seemed ta ooze dru' every crack,
> And though there weren't no chain to pull, we never felt the lack,
> A candle in a jamjar were our only bit of light;
> It came in very handy when old Nature called at night!
> To add to the excitement as you sat there in the dark
> A large fat hairy spider on some errand might embark;

He'd swing about quite gaily clinging to his silken thread
As hypnotised you watched and prayed,
'Please, don't fall on me yud.'
Ay, many were the pleasant hours spent there in reverie,
Gone now, but not forgotten – THAT OLD OUTSIDE WC

The best public loo in the Nepalese Himalayas!

A FEW WORDS

ON CHAMBER POTS

The chamber pot is one of the oldest utensils of civilization. Pieces of pots have been found in Egyptian Pharoahs' tombs.

And utensils shaped like a sauce-boat, called *Bourdalous*, were invented in the first place to relieve the ladies of the Court of King Louis XIV, in late-seventeenth-century France. They took their name from the King's Jesuit Court Preacher, Louis Bourdaloue, whose marathon sermons had the women riveted to the church pews.

I wonder where and when they got rid of the contents of their Bourdalous?

In Munich a man called Manfred Klauda has set up what must be the world's first chamber pot museum. His collection to date is of 5,000 pots, with 600 on permanent display. Included in the collection is a two thousand-year-old Roman green glass urine bottle. There are musical ones and useful ones – like the German one which was made during the first world war and inscribed:

Push and strain with all your might
and help the farmer in his plight·

Another use for an old bedpan – pot pourri

Witty chamber pot

And a silver one engraved with these words:

From little streams do great rivers flow

By 1880 many jerry pots or chamber pots were most elaborate, even to the extent of portraits in the bottom of them. Some manufacturers used the face of Napoleon in theirs, others had an eye painted in them along with ribald rhymes, like:

When you use me keep me clean
And I won't tell you what I have seen

Did you know that in bygone days in the House of Commons a silver pot was fitted in the Speaker's Chair to allow him to relieve himself and to be present throughout parliamentary debates?

The final word on chamber pots deserves to go to a correspondent from Suffolk, who sent in this story:

Sarah Green was very fat – never weighed 'erself mind, but 'er must 'ave been twenty stone if 'ere was a pound. Bad 'a-bed 'er was with 'er tenth child, and course 'er couldn't get down to the earth closet at the bottom of the garden.

The local woman, Mrs Allsop, who was in charge of the 'atching and despatchin' in the village, was looking after 'er.

'You'll have to try and go, missus', she said to Sarah, ''tis four days now, and I shall have to give you a dose of liquid paraffin if you don't perform today.'

Liquid paraffin was summit that Sarah hated, so as soon as Mrs Allsop had gone downstairs to see to the other children, Sarah climbs out of bed and fetches the chamber-pot out from underneath it, and sets on 'im. Suddenly, there was a terrible noise along with screechin' and a-hollering.

Mrs Allsop rushed upstairs to find Sarah sprawled on the floor surrounded by pee and poop and broken pieces of

The author, head through a one-holer, surrounded by jerry pots

crock – her weight had broke the chamber pot, spilling the contents all over the floor, and to make matters worse Sarah's backside was cut to pieces and bleeding summut terrible.

Then there was the job of getting 'er up and into bed. Mrs Allsop had to send for Sarah's husband, a farm worker 'e was, and his boss didn't think much of it – one of his workers going home in the middle of the morning and they in the middle of lambing too.

Mind you, Sarah should have 'ad the doctor to stitch up 'er backside, but a doctor's visit had to be paid for in they days, and 'er husband's wages was only twenty-five shillings a week, so 'er had to put up with it.

Mrs Allsop came up with a good idea, 'er brought some biggish bath towels from home and put them on Sarah, like you would a baby's napkin.

And for some time till her backside healed, that's what Sarah had to do; wear a nappy, made 'er look fatter than ever, it did, 'er used to waddle about like an outsized duck.

Appendix II

OUR PRIVY HERITAGE

The subject of privies and early places of conveniences seems to fascinate most people, and thankfully several museums in Britain have preserved some of these, most of which can be seen on display, or on request. Here is a list of some of the museums and public places where they can be found:

Iron Bridge Gorge Museum

At the Iron Bridge Gorge Museum at Telford, in their 'Blists Hill Open Air Museum', they have (non-working) earth closets on display adjacent to the Squatters Cottage and the Shelton Toll House. They also have 'Turn of the Century' toilets at the rear of their re-erected Public House on the same site. In the museum library, they have several ironmongers' catalogues etc. which depict early water closets.

Salford Art Gallery & Museum

The Keeper of the Social History at The City of Salford Art Gallery and Museum sent this list of items that they have there, although not necessarily on display. However anyone wishing to study this sort of thing would be welcome to do so, by arrangement. They note that 'items in the collection for which we have catalogue cards' are as follows:

Bed pans: The New Slipper, 2 (739–1959 & H139–1975)
Stoneware specimen (550–1966)
Enamel specimen (H177–1976)
Ideal bed and douche slipper (H453–1981)

Chamber pots: Pottery. Reg. 330769 (1899 +)
Pottery with pansy decoration
Pair of decorated pots (part of toilet set): The Foley semi-porcelain England Rd. 330395 (1926–30 +) (498–1966/6)
18th-century decorated marriage gift. Inscriptions:
(1) Marriage/This post is a present sent/some mirth to make is only Meant/We hope the same you'll not refuse/But keep it safe and oft it Use/When in it you want to P-ss, Remember them who sent you THIS!
(2) A blessing on you both i give/Long and happy may you live/May discord never be your lot/But virtue reign within your cot.
(3) Inside: A moulded applied frog on side. Painted transfer print of cross-legged man on bottom with two word balloons: 'Oh! dear me' 'What do I see' and legend 'Keep me clean and use me well/And what I see I will not tell'.

Commodes: Armchair/commode with cane seat which lifts
              up to form commode.
              Child's chair/commode, oak (H90–1980).
              Child's rocking chair, commode type. Early
              19th century (79–1957).
              Mahogany commode with earthenware bowl
              (625–1973).
              Travelling carriage commode i.e. bowl in box,
              c.1900 (466–1972).

Lavatory chain handle 'PULL' (627–1973)
Lavatory chain handle, blue earthenware (628–1973)
Lavatory chain handle, pottery (PP1973–73).

Duckett's 4–gallon patent tipper (744–1970)
Fowler's patent tipper, post 1874 (H126–1982)

Water closets: Baxendales perfect flush out. White pottery
              basin on back of reclining lion (28–1965)
              'The New Argosy' Toilet pan used in schools
              (626–1973)
              'Cambridge' Rd nos. 173766 & 206804 (1891 &
              1893)

Trade catalogue for Baxendale & Co. Ltd., Miller Street,
Manchester, *c*.1920 'Catalogue of Baths, Lavatories, sinks,
sanitary ware and appliances for the plumbing and decorating
trades'. This includes sections on closets, urinals, flushing
cisterns and illustrations of bathrooms (24–1969).

Earth closet, with a hopper at the back for ashes or earth

Beamish, North of England Open Air Museum, Stanley, Co. Durham

They provided this information:

> We have in the open air museum a number of 'netties' or earth closets, some preserved on their original site, others reconstructed. There is a two-holer at the Home Farm and other earth closets at the pit cottages. We have also a rather splendid example of a 'Doultons Lambeth Patent Pedestal Combination Flushout closet' in one of our town houses. Apart from the above mentioned items we have a number of closets, beautifully decorated in store as well as the more utilitarian Revd. Moule's type of patent. We also have a library and photographic archive which includes some very interesting illustrations.

Museum of Sheffield, City Museum, Weston Park, Sheffield

The Keeper of Social and Labour history provided further information on privies:

> Although we have a few washdown closets, these are in store at Kelham Island Industrial Museum and can only be seen by appointment as we do not have a social history gallery in Sheffield. There is an earth closet at Abbeydale Industrial Hamlet and a close stool in the bedchamber at Bishops' House.

Contents of an early bathroom – note the bidet on the right

Museum of East Anglian Life, Stowmarket

Here they have a reconstructed mill and millhouse on-site, complete with outside privy. This is a two-seater and is flushed with an overflow of water from the mill pond. They also have examples of jug and bowl sets and chamber pots in their ironmonger's shop and another complete set in their bedroom display. In the Domestic Life building is a large mobile bath with iron wheels that was used in a workhouse near Woodbridge and an earth/sand closet, made of wood with a high back, of the type that dispenses sand from a hopper.

Gladstone Pottery Museum, Longton, Stoke-on-Trent

The Sanitary Ceramics Gallery of the Gladstone Museum concentrates mostly on early water closets, and have a wonderful display of these, and of how these early lavatory pans were made. They also hand visitors a copy of their booklet entitled *Water Closets, Past, Present & Future* which covers all sorts of details including things like the 'longpot or hopper closet, slop water and tipper closets, pan and washdown closets'.

York Castle Museum

The Keeper of Social History at the York Castle Museum says that there is much to see. They have a good collection of water closets and privies, a range which are on display, including:

A two-seater earth privy
Revd Moule's earth closet

Author's temporary collection of privies at Cogges Museum, Witney

A pan closet, early 1900s

A valve closet, 1890

Two washdown closets, one with an S-bend, built 1805

A close stool pot and a selection of early toilet rolls and chains

A delightful chamber pot with these words around the flat rim:

> 'Hand it over to me, my dear'.

Also a separate display called 'Past Exhibition of Household History'.

PRIVIES GALORE

Avoncroft Museum of Buildings, Stoke Heath, Bromsgrove

Michael Thomas, Curator of Avoncroft, is delighted to show visitors the splendid ancient three-holer that he and his staff rescued from the garden of a grand house in Leominster. It was taken down brick-by-brick and re-erected at Avoncroft, and is a grand privy from a grand house – not the usual country three-holer.

Norwich Bridewell Museum

Sanitary ware:

Commode, Dutch, *c.* 1780 (443.970)

Commode, mahogany, late 18th/early 19th century (213.975.73)

China bedpan, 'The Ideal Bed and Douche Slipper', early 20th century (92.975.9)

Chamber pot (child's), late 19th century (758.968)

Chamber pot, stoneware with conical tin lid, from the Bridewell Walsingham, Norfolk, 19th century (191.971.2)

Enamel chamber pot & commode from workhouse at Pulham, Norfolk, late 19th century (371.973.28 & 371.973.14)

Lavatory seat, double, North Norfolk, early 19th century (38.970)

Lavatory seat, double, North Norfolk (Wells), early 20th century (167.975.20)

Cistern, *The Burlington*, pat. no. 374873, late 19th century (172.978)

Cistern, Tylors, London, Sydney. 'Column' reg. no. 151483 (53.980)

Bowl, 'George Jennings Patentee Stangate London', *c*. 1880
(333.985)
Novio & *Bromo* lavatory paper 1890–1910 (634.974)
Cistern & seat with retailer's mark: Chas. Holborn & Co.,
Norwich (423.977)

And there is also a seventeenth-century privy that was found
when the site for a large supermarket was being excavated in
Norwich.

Appendix III

MEDICINES OF OLD

From Abbot Feckenham's *Booke of sovereigne medicines
againste the most common and knowne diseases, chiefly for the
poor, who have not at all times the learned phisitions at hande*,
1515–84.

A medecyne to purge the bladder of him that cannot pisse
Take fennell the leaves and the rootes, alleydanders, parceley the
leaves and the rootes, hartstonnge, mayden heare, and seethe
them in white wyne, and give it to the patient to drinke. It shall
purge the bladder in short tyme.

An easy purgation
Take a pynte of white wyne, one ounce of serce and a goode
handfull of reysons of he sonne, the stones beinge takinge out,
and a halfe sponefull and annyseedes. Put all theis in the said
white wyne a whole nighte, and the nexte morninge, boile it to a
draught, and soe let the patient drinke it blood warme. And yf
you will you maie putt thereinto iii or iiii rootes of polipodion of
the oke.

For bellie trobled with wynde, gapynes or gnawings

Take culver donnge, brayed finelie and sodd in a pynte of white wyne, and uppon a cleane cloathe laye it playster weise uppon yr bellie and it shall expell the wynde and payne thereof.

For the same

Take a good quanteitie of plantyne leaves and beinge verye well sodd, put it into a close stoole, and sit thereon, that maieste receive the ayre thereof uppwarde into thy bodye and it takethe awaye the payne of the bellie incontinent.

For the flixe of the bellie

Let the patient receive from under a close stole, or suche like, the smoke of rustic iron of burnyng heate, quenched in vinaigre. Also culver dounge stampt and used for a playster with strong vinagre, and applied to the bellie navell byndeth incontinent all Flixe of the bellie.